"Global Doodle Gems" Easter Collection Volume 1

Drawn & colored by Maud Feral Chauveau (MFC)

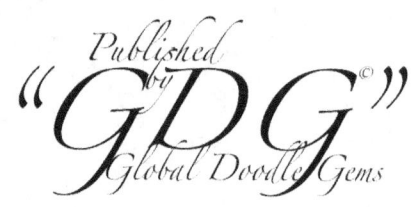

Share your colored versions with us ! We love seeing your results and hearing from you we are social !

The Official FB book page, stay on top of what we have in the works !
www.facebook.com/globaldoodlegems

The Community group, share your colored pages, meet the artists, enjoy exclusive freebies, take part in community Charity books and so much more......
www.facebook.com/groups/globaldoodlegems/

Follow us on Twitter.... @GlobalDoodlegem

We are on Instagram too
@globaldoodlegems for instagram

...and if you are not social like that we have a blog
globaldoodlegems.wordpress.com

Copyright © 2015 Global Doodle Gems

All rights are reserved by Global Doodle Gems.

Duplication of pages for personal use are allowed. You are invited to color the pages then scan/post your coloured versions to social networks, mentioning the book title and author/artist (Global Doodle Gems).

All artwork and images are protected by copyright laws. This book or any portion thereof may not, otherwise, be reproduced and/or distributed or transmitted without the express written permission of the artist/publisher of Global Doodle Gems.

All of us from the Global Doodle Gems wish you a colortastic time and look forward to seeing your wonderful color results online !

Contributing artists

Johanna Ans, Jane Levi, Rover Hsiao,
T.J., Yaya, Creative Rosalien,
Pica Wu, Alfred E. Villanueva,
Jenny Wei, Jennifer Rainbow Beryllium,
Audrey Sagh, Joann Sands,
Iben Lykke Højholdt, Nancy43,
L'aety Esperanza,, Debbie Lai,
Neeti Goswami, Maud Feral Chauveau (MFC),
Orbleue's, Marie-Eve Klein,
Mireille Westerduin, Colour by Mi,
Ellen Wolters, Ondine Summers,
Peggy Sue's Artwork, Nicole Whelan,
Adriana Graciela Volpe, Hung Ai-Ling,
Arianne Schimmel, Isa Humeau,
Heather Richards, Sabine Design,
Laurie Beauchamp, Jovian Ke,
Wenyu Lin Small Fish, Angel Huang,
Les galaxies de 'Qi, Wen Kung,
Linda Fauconnier Tricoire, Gemeta Ling
&
Maria Wedel

Contributing Artist
MWMS-Johanna Ans
The Netherlands

Blog : mywaymystylejohannaans.wordpress.com

Facebook : Johanna-Ans-My-creative-site

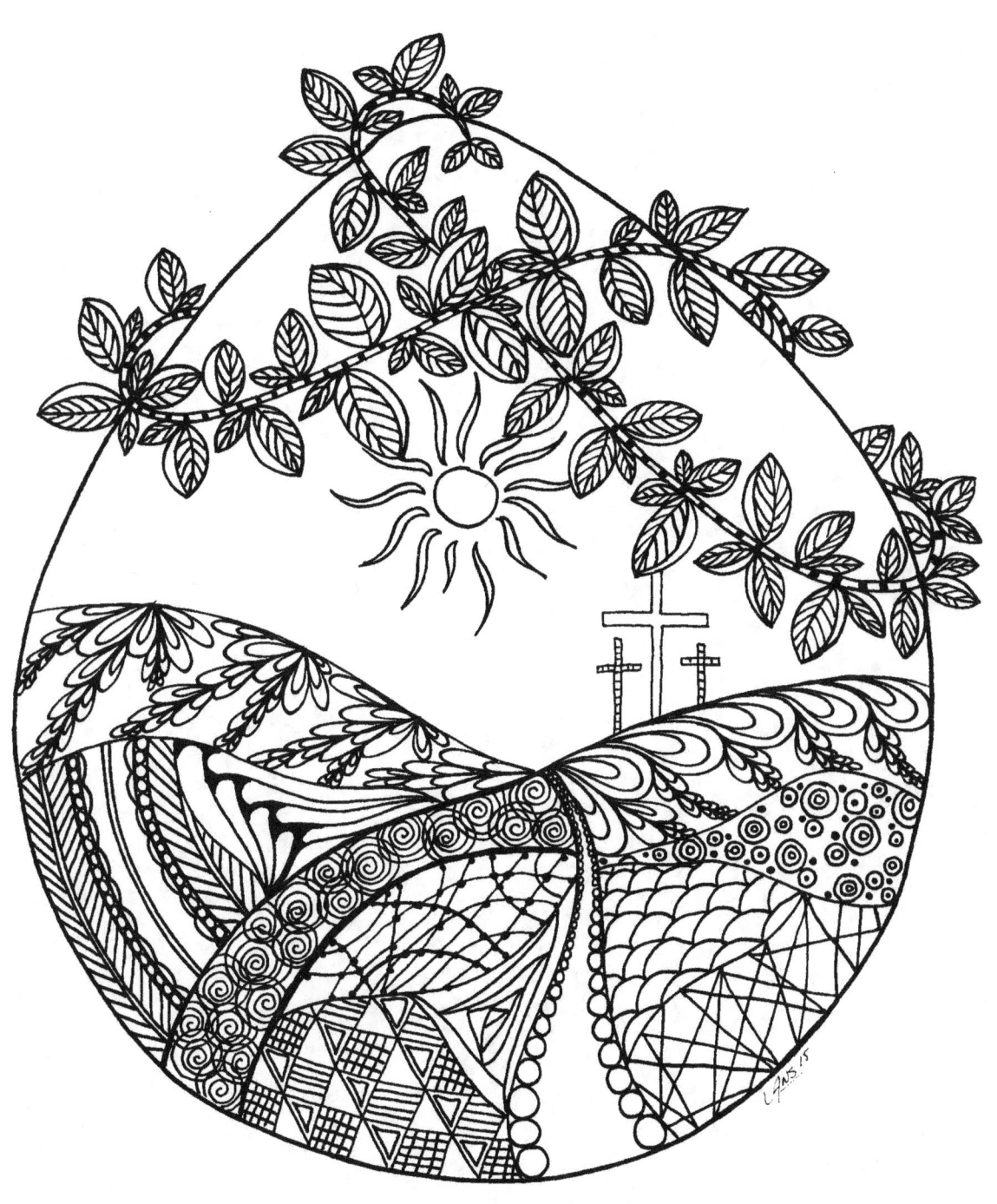

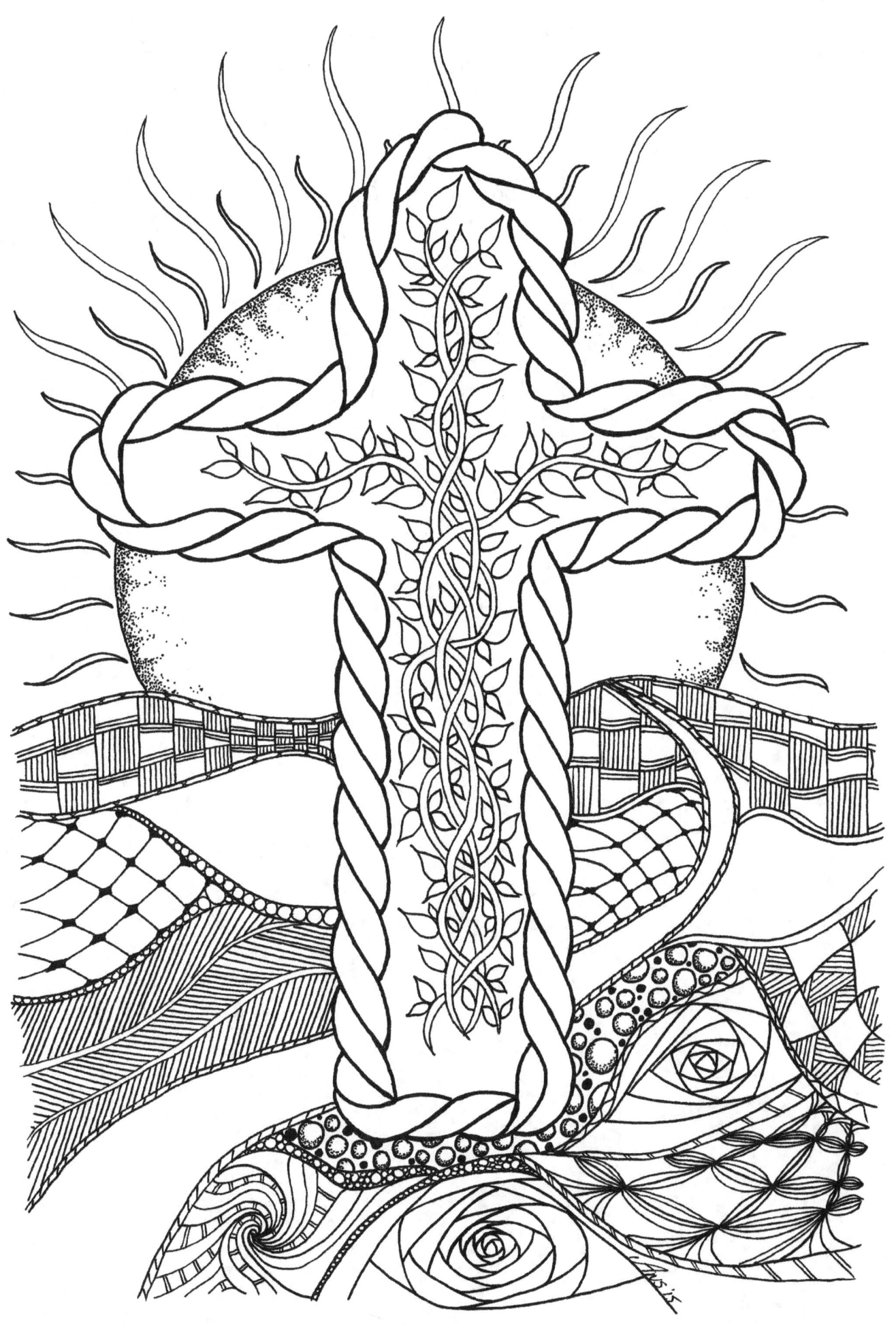

Contributing Artist
Jane Levi
France

Facebook : Cheeky-Cats

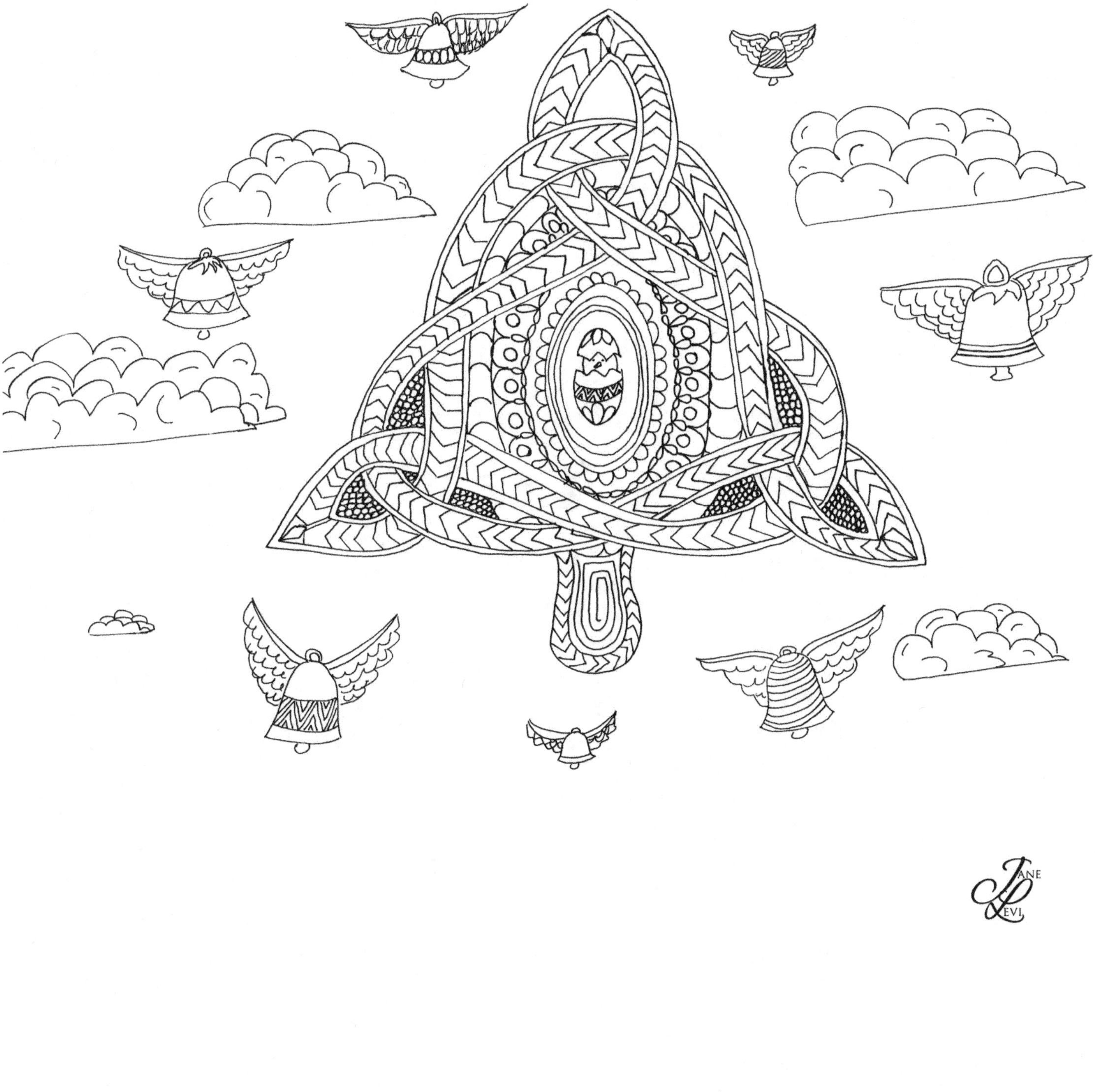

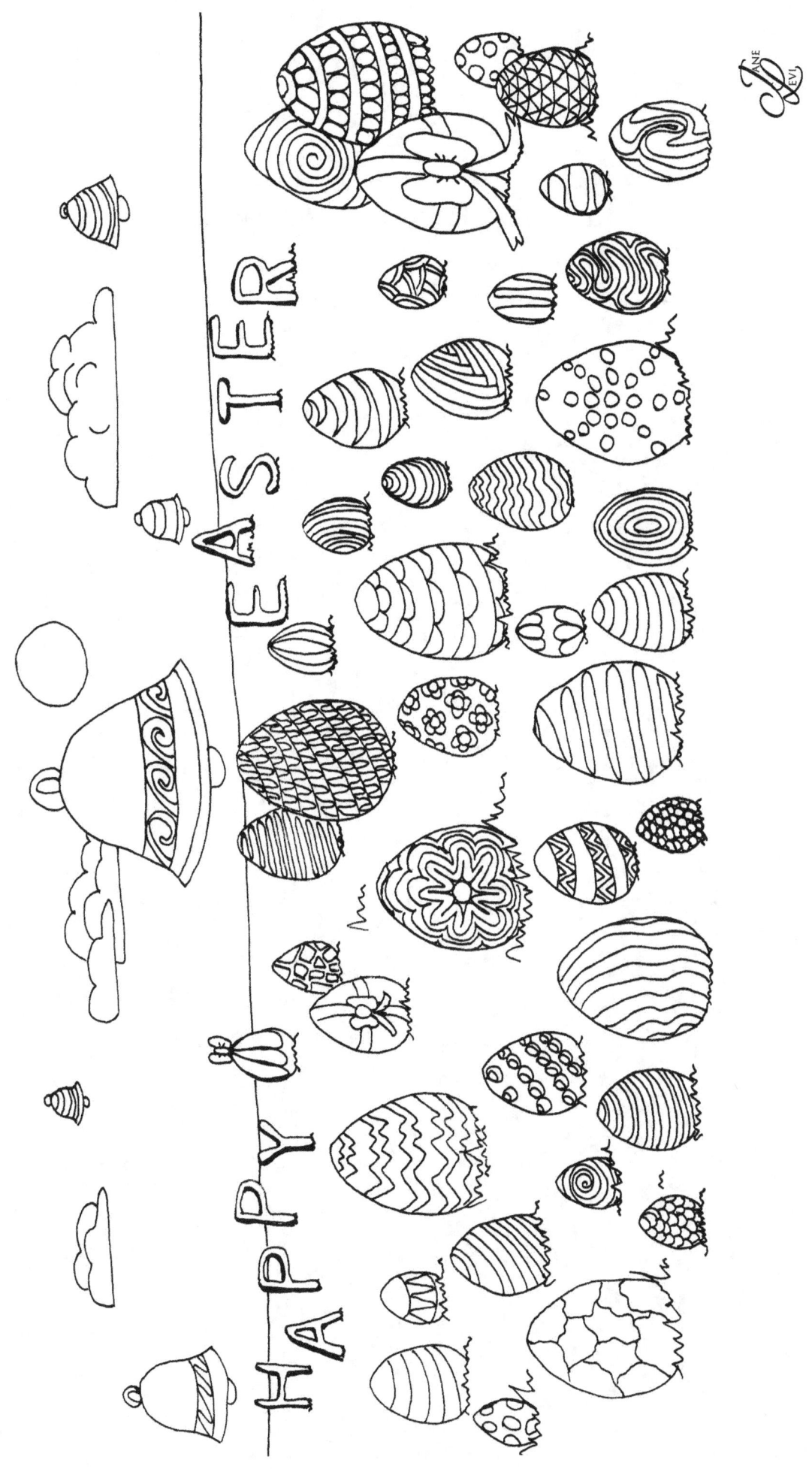

Contributing Artist
Rover Hsiao
Taiwan

Facebook : roverhsiao2015

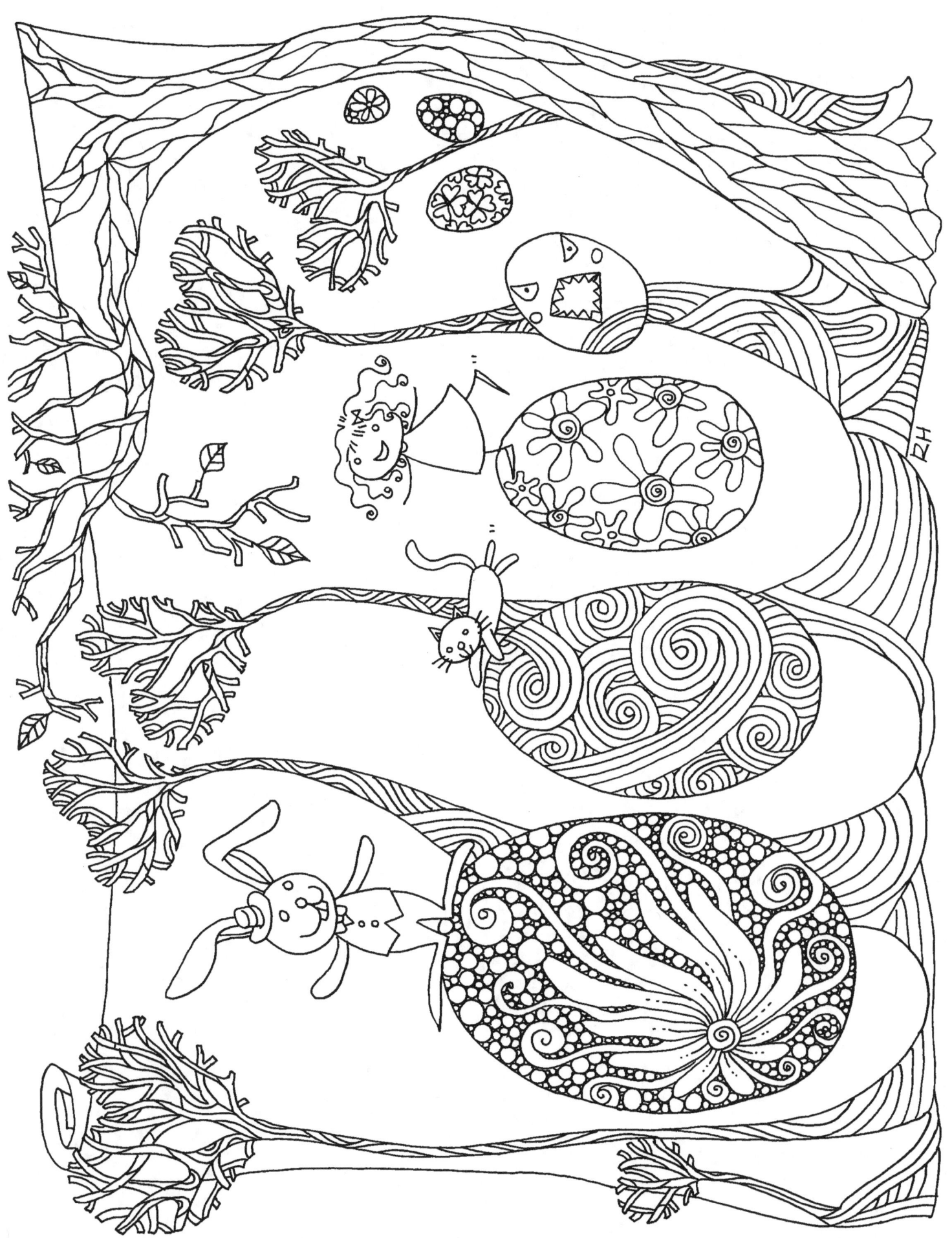

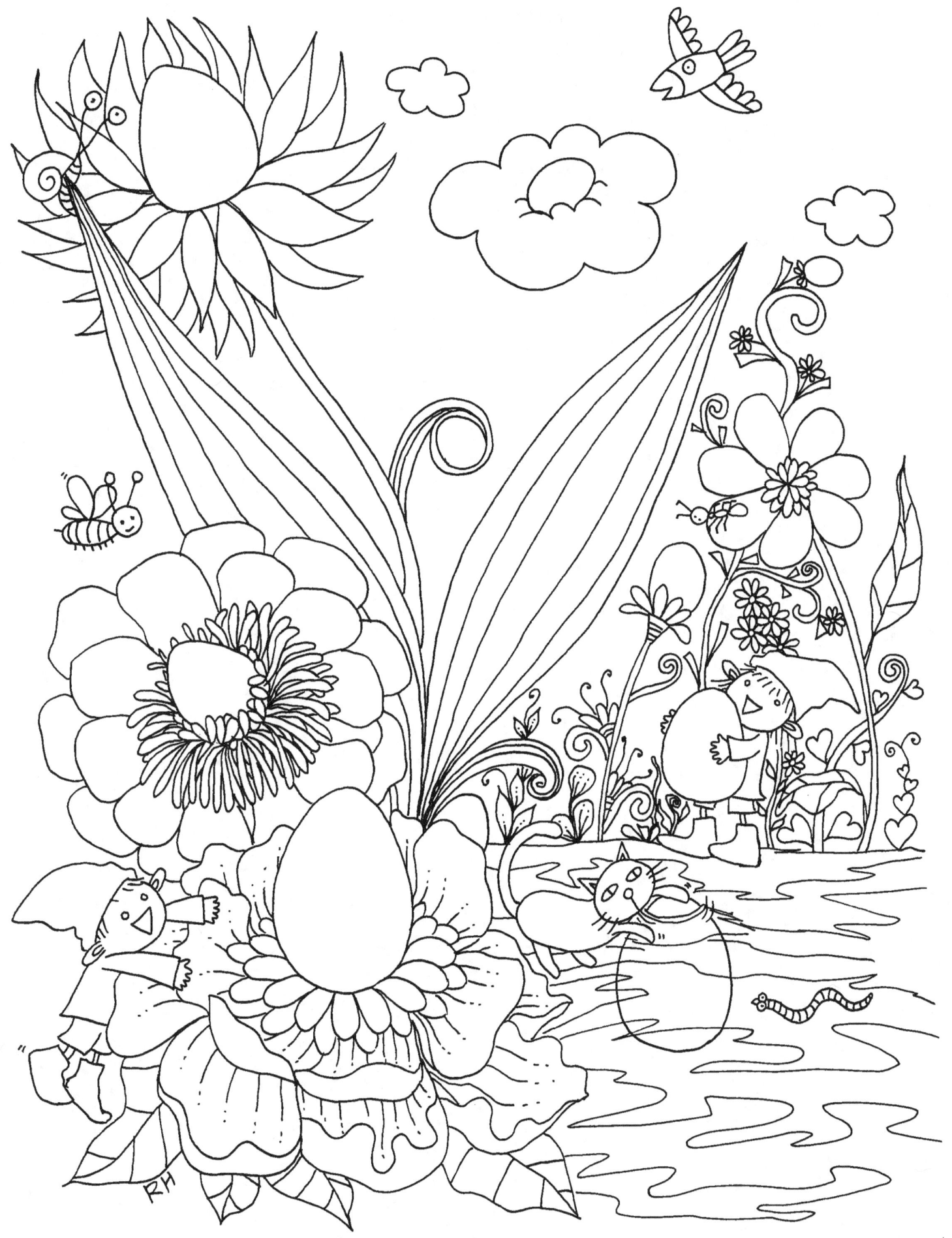

Contributing Artist
T.J.
USA

Facebook : TJsArtCorner

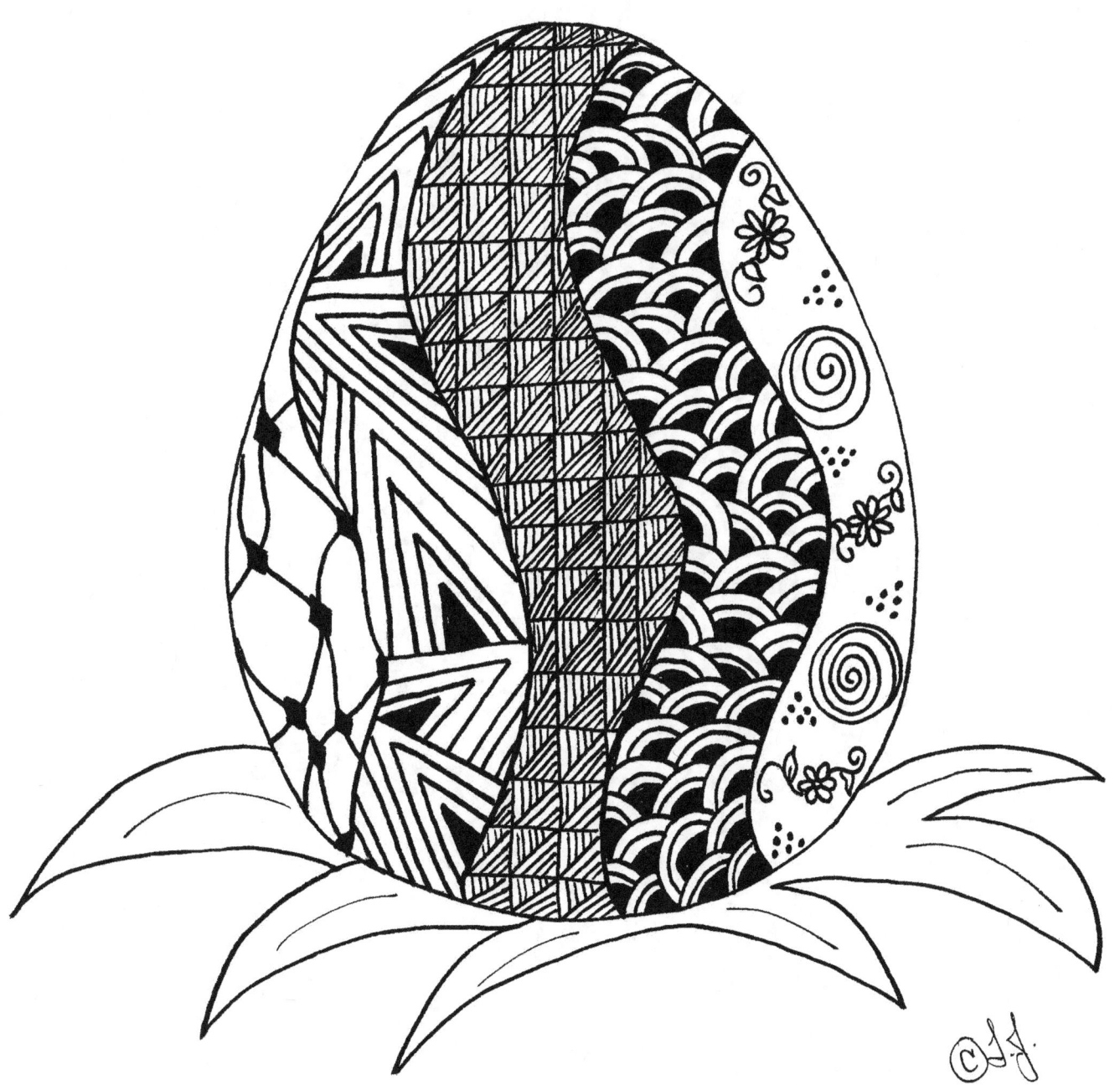

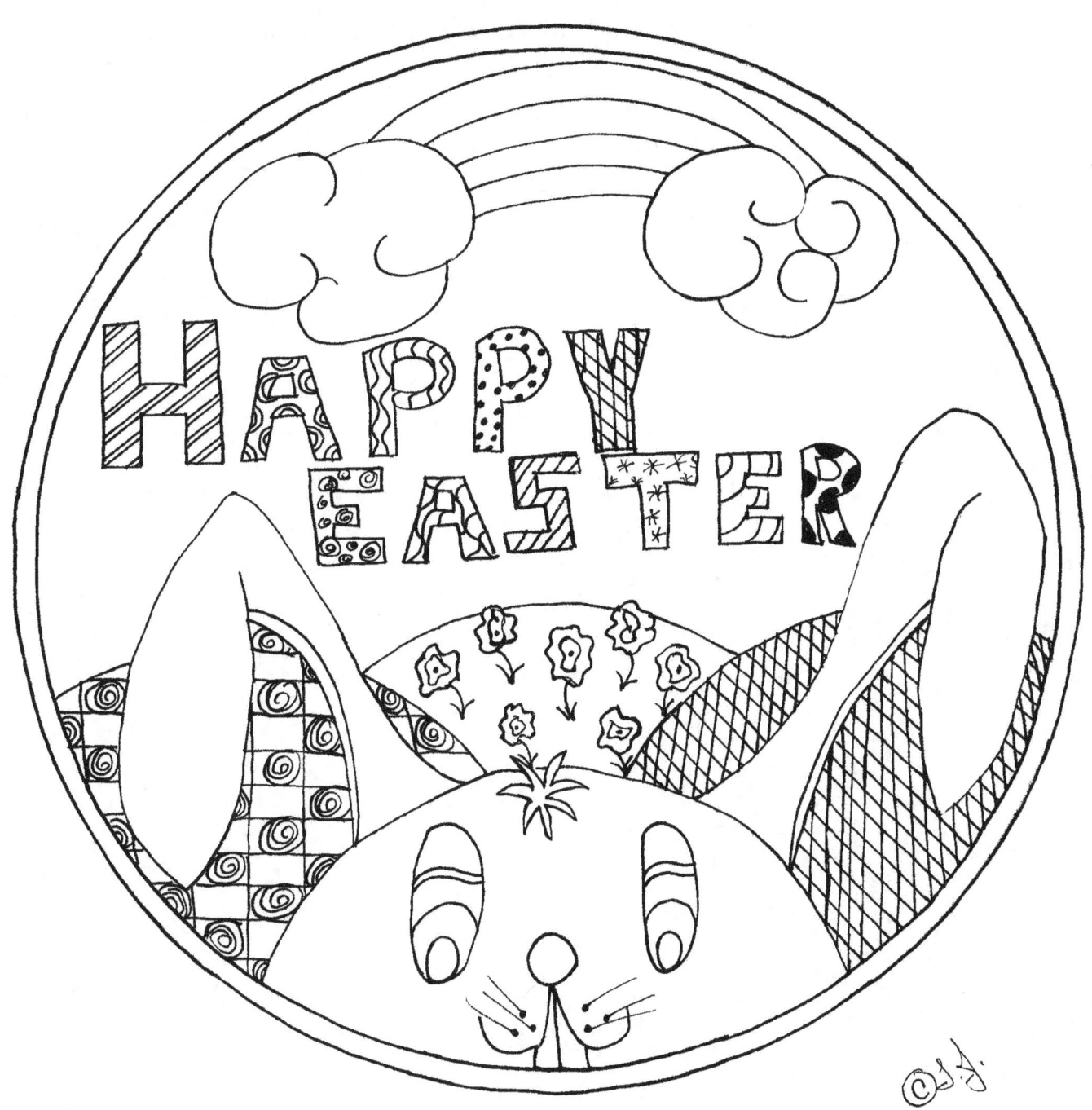

Contributing Artist
Yaya
France

Facebook : Les-gribouillis-de-yaya-georgia-merino

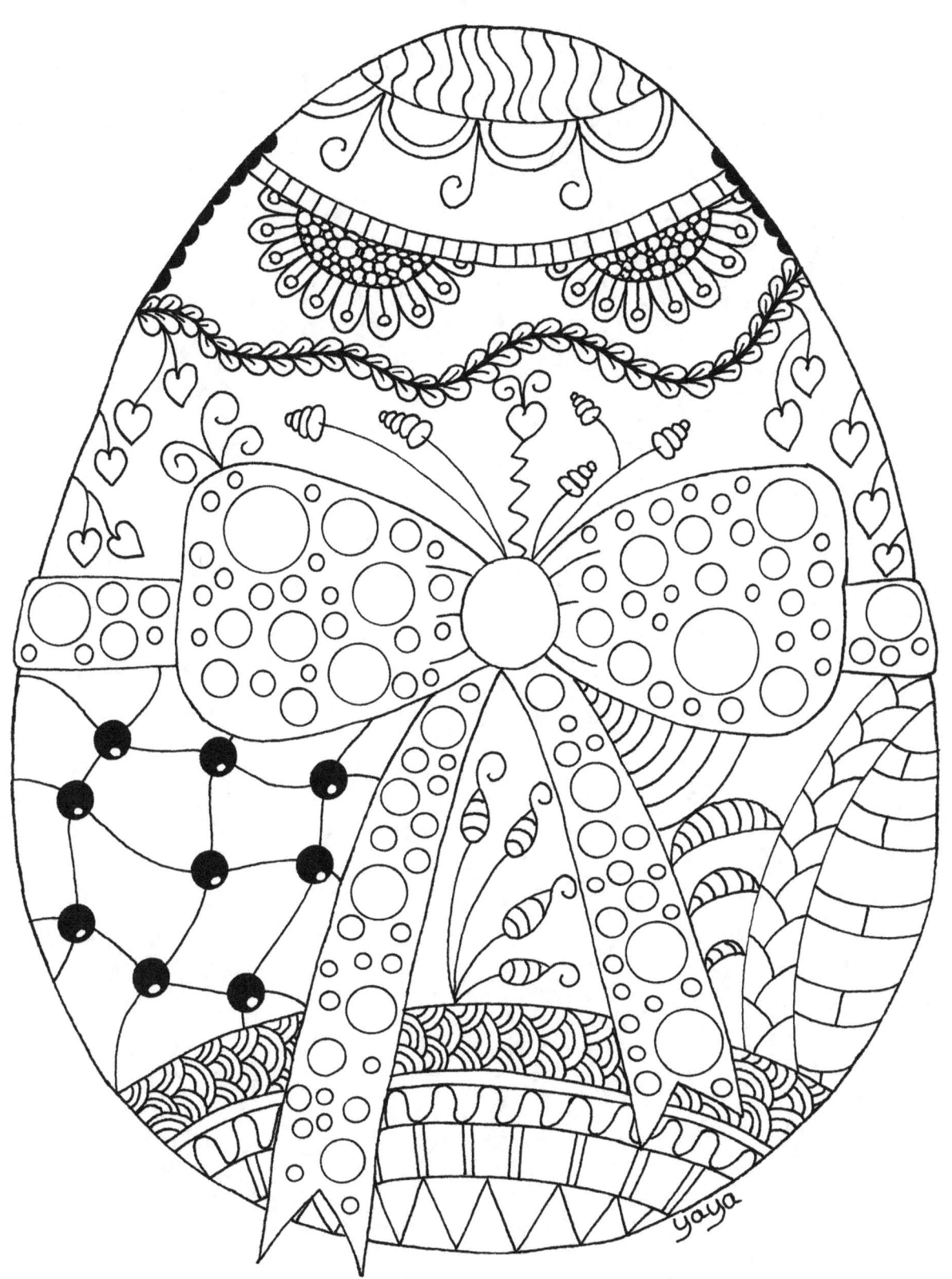

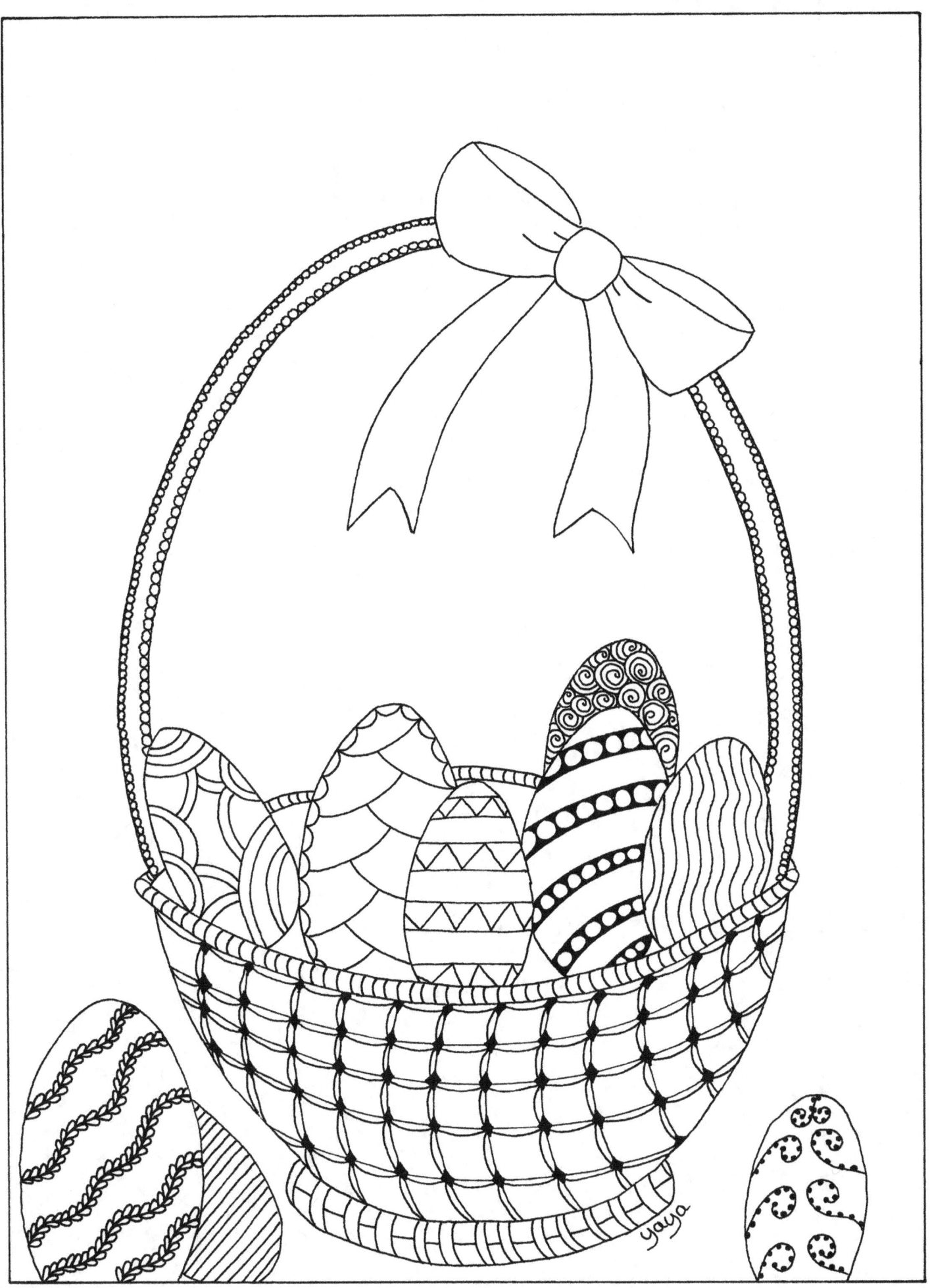

Contributing Artist
Creative Rosalien
Norway

Facebook : Creative Rosalien

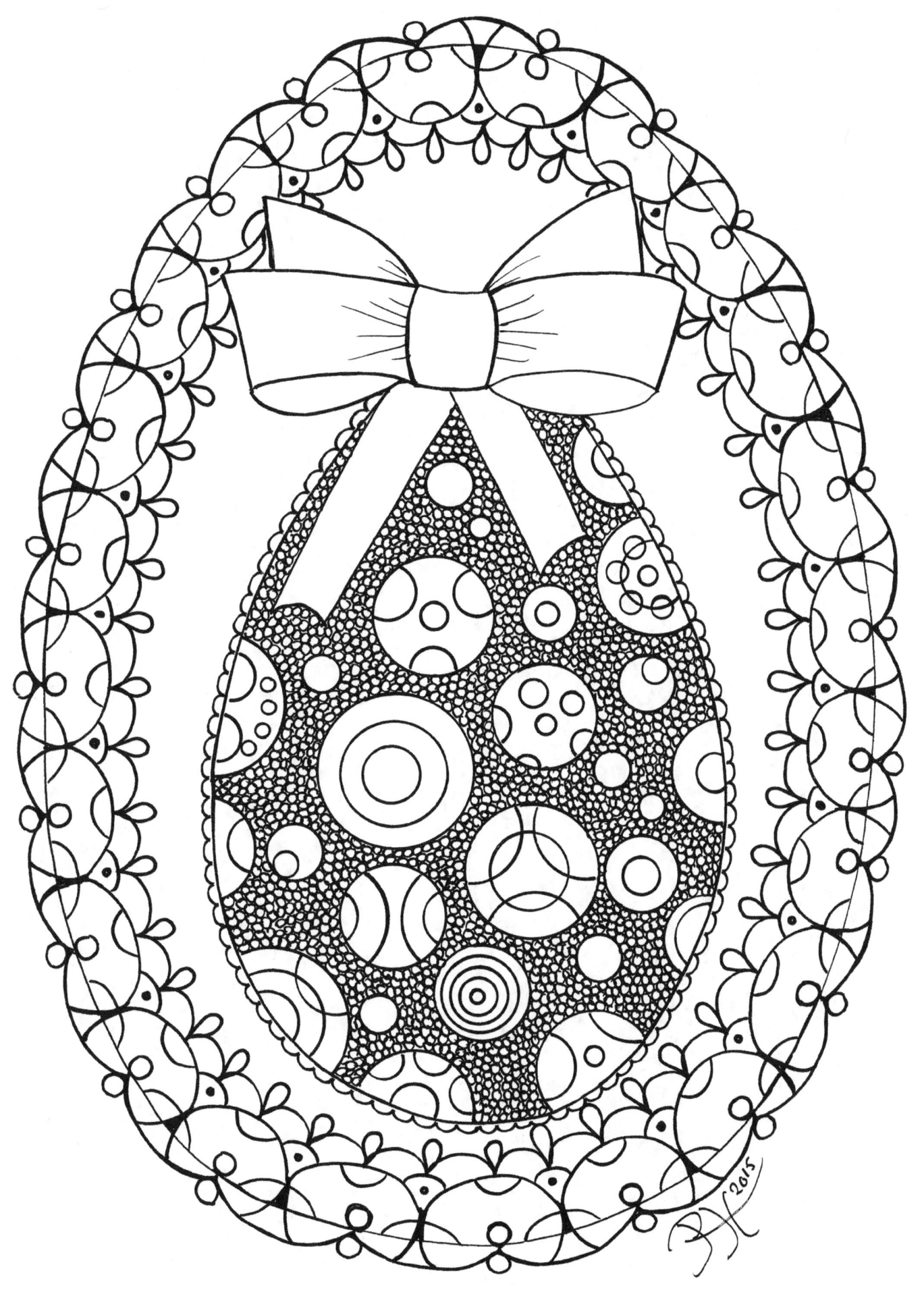

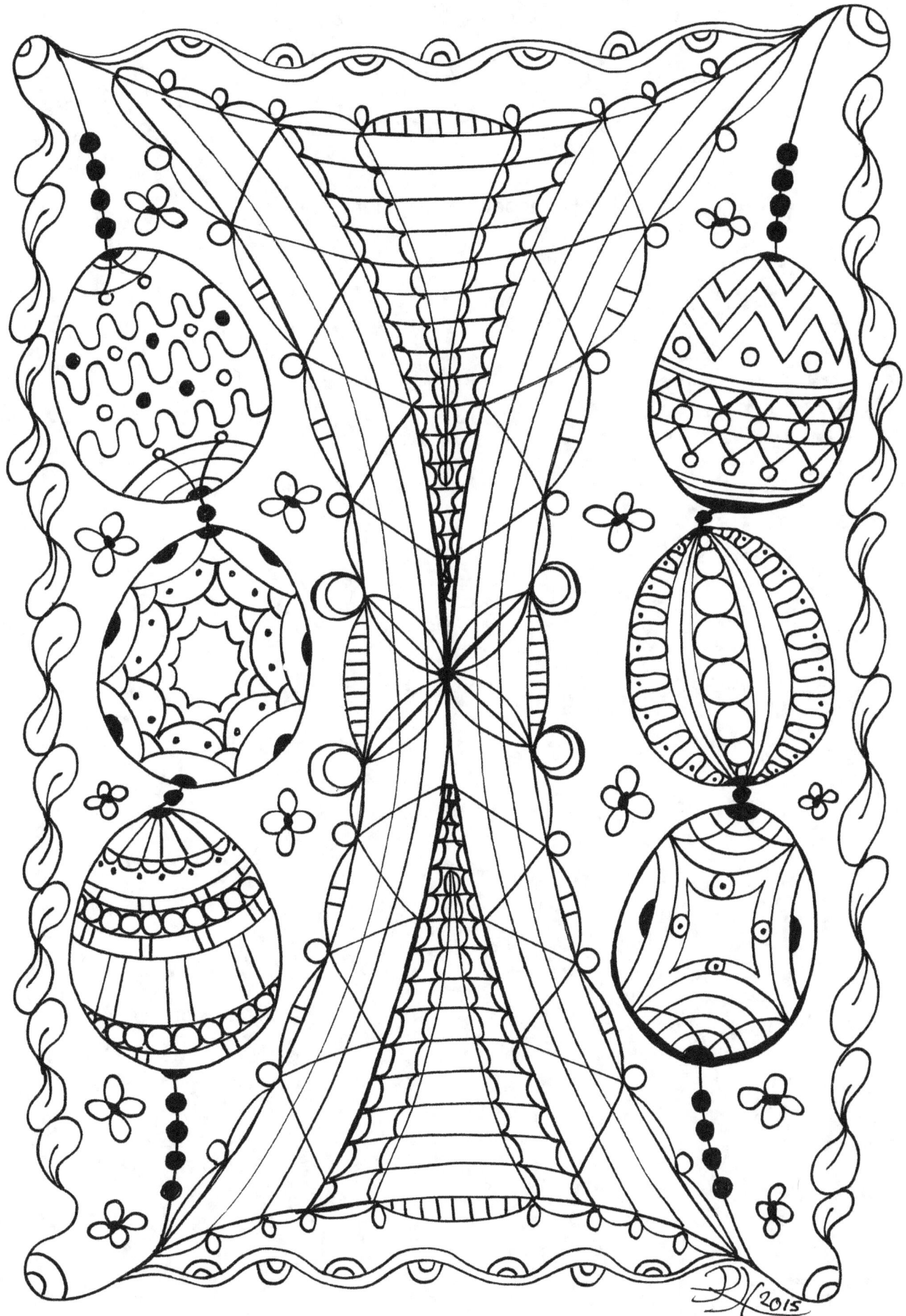

Contributing Artist
Pica Wu
Taiwan

Facebook : picapicadrow2

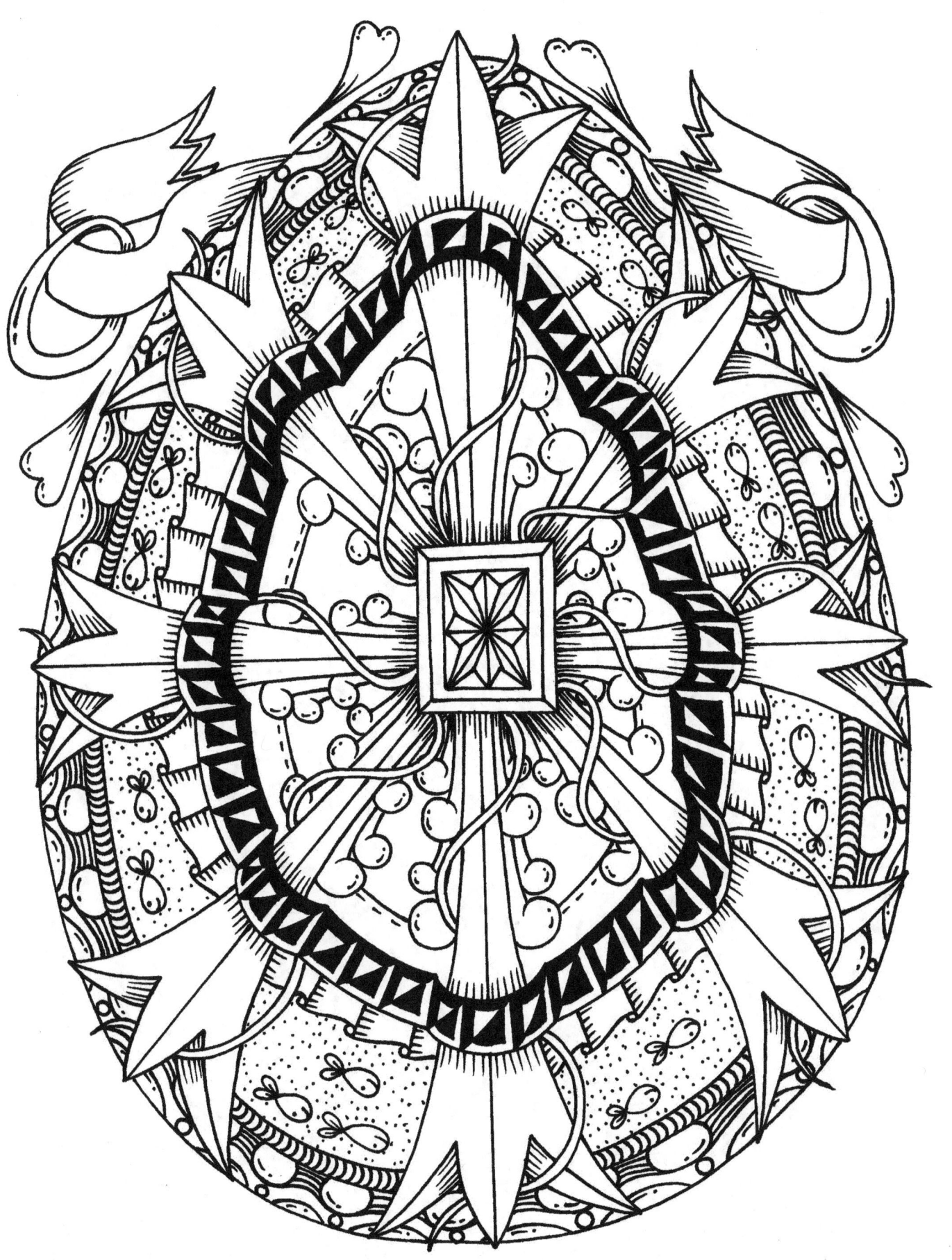

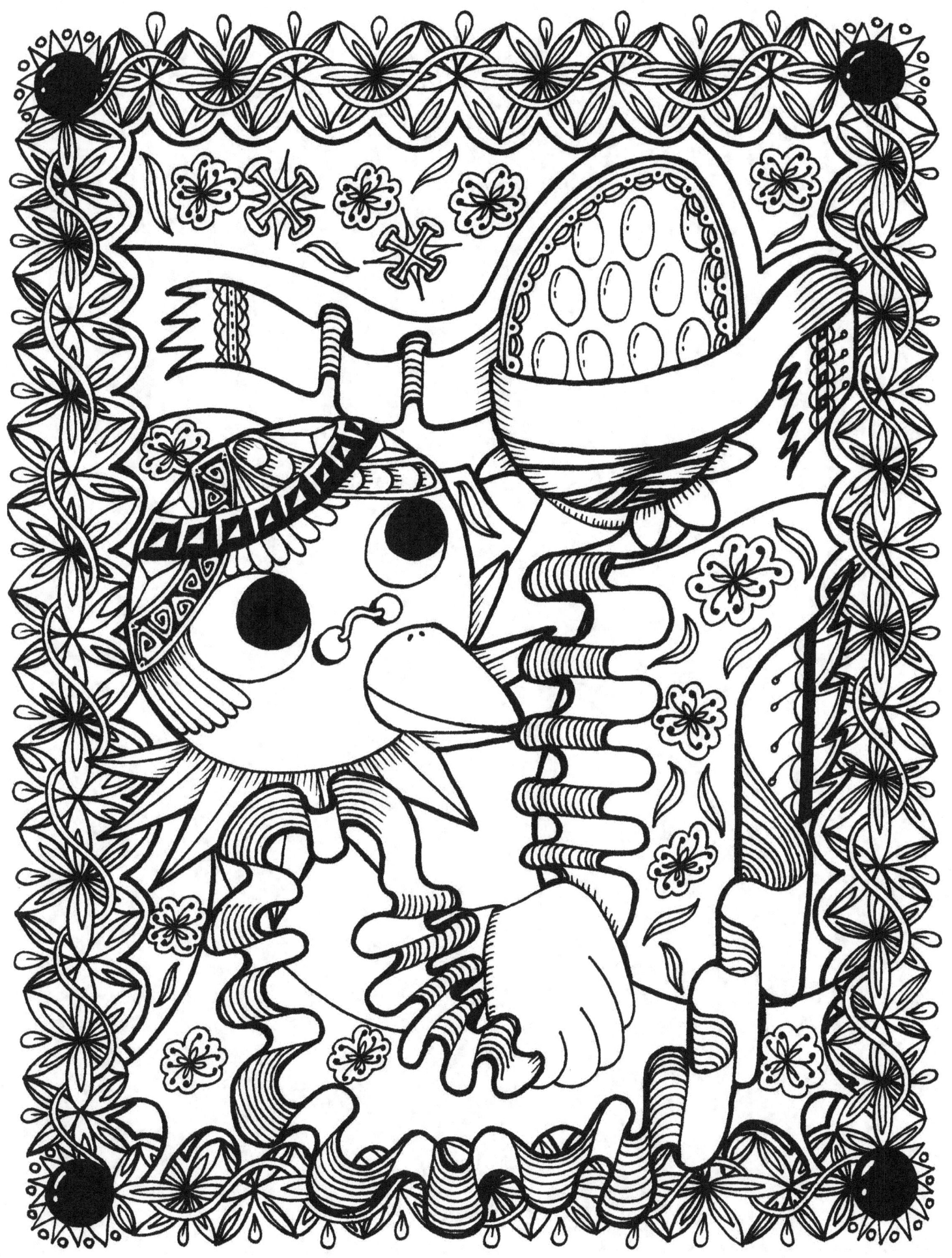

Contributing Artist
Alfred E. Villanueva
Philippines
Facebook : viworksart2015

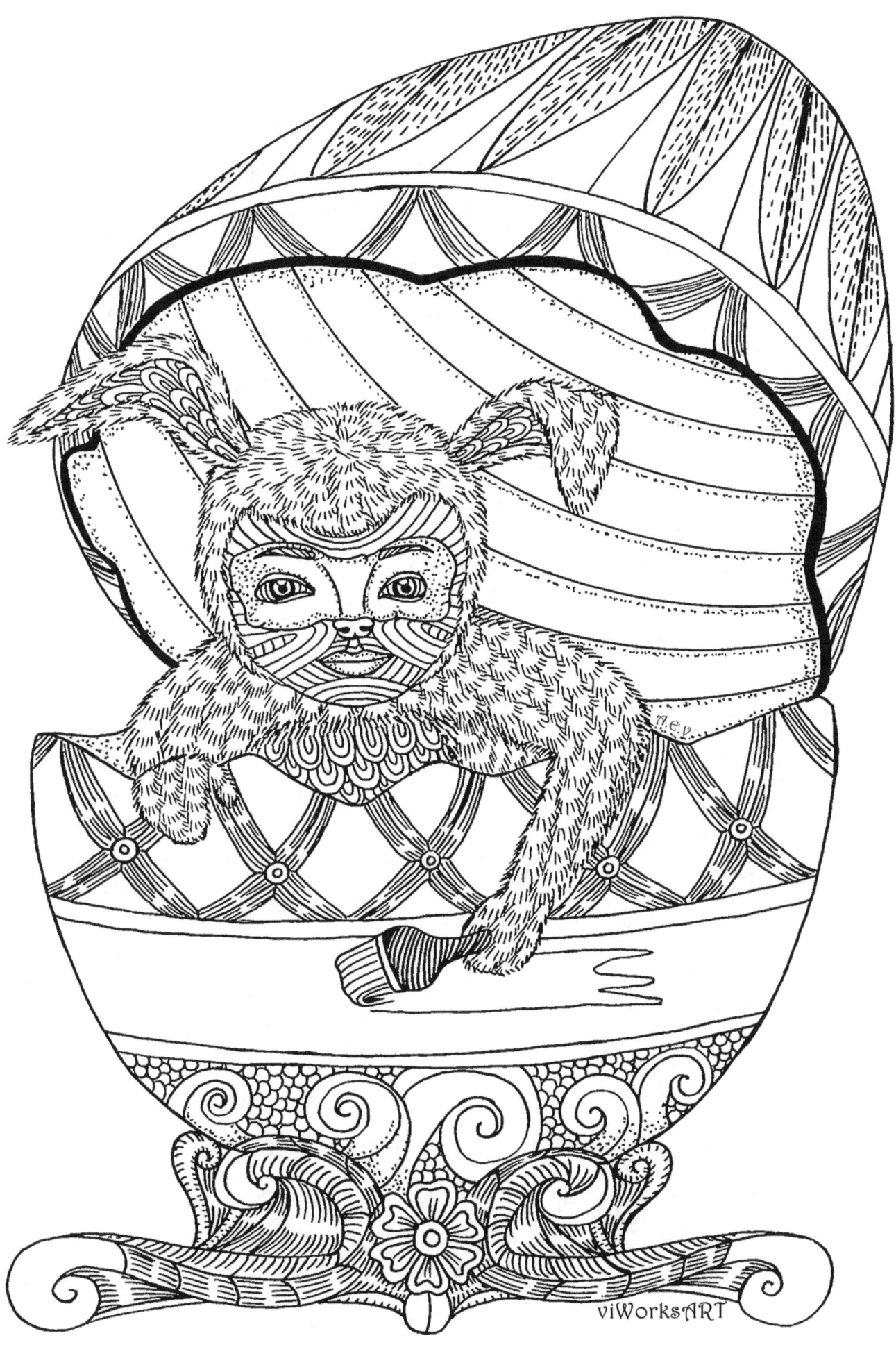

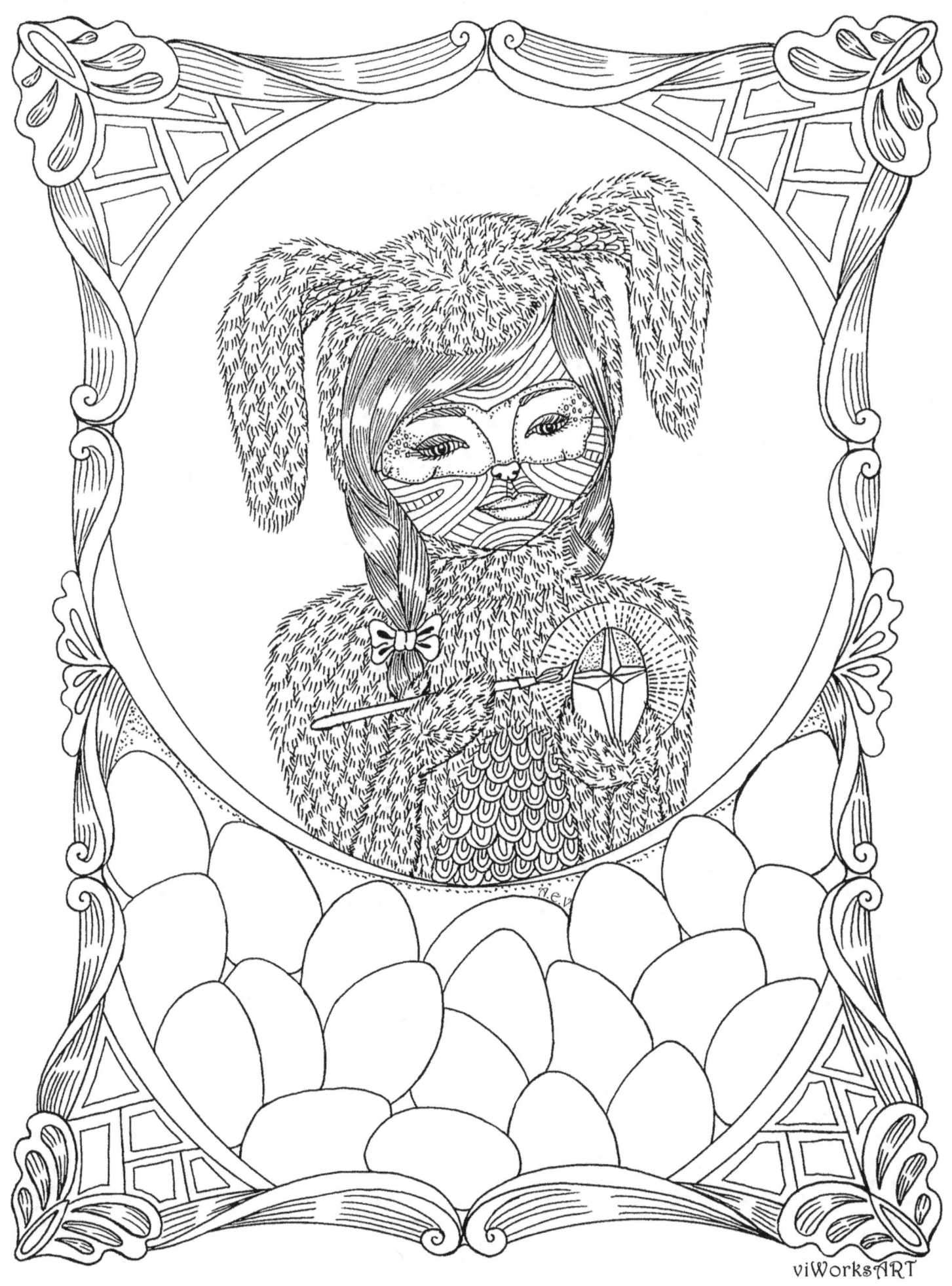

Contributing Artist
Jenny Wei
Taiwan

Facebook : zentanglefun

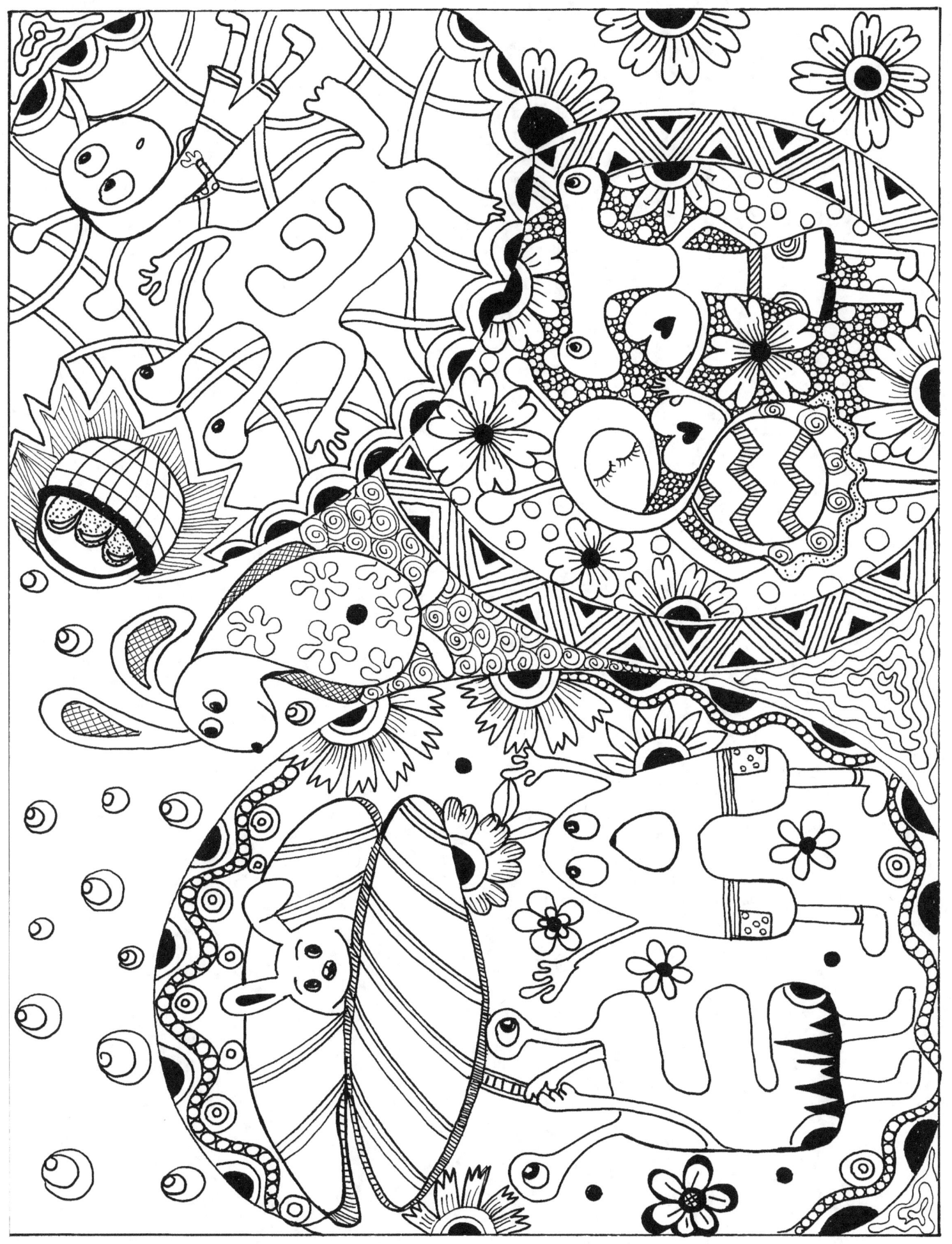

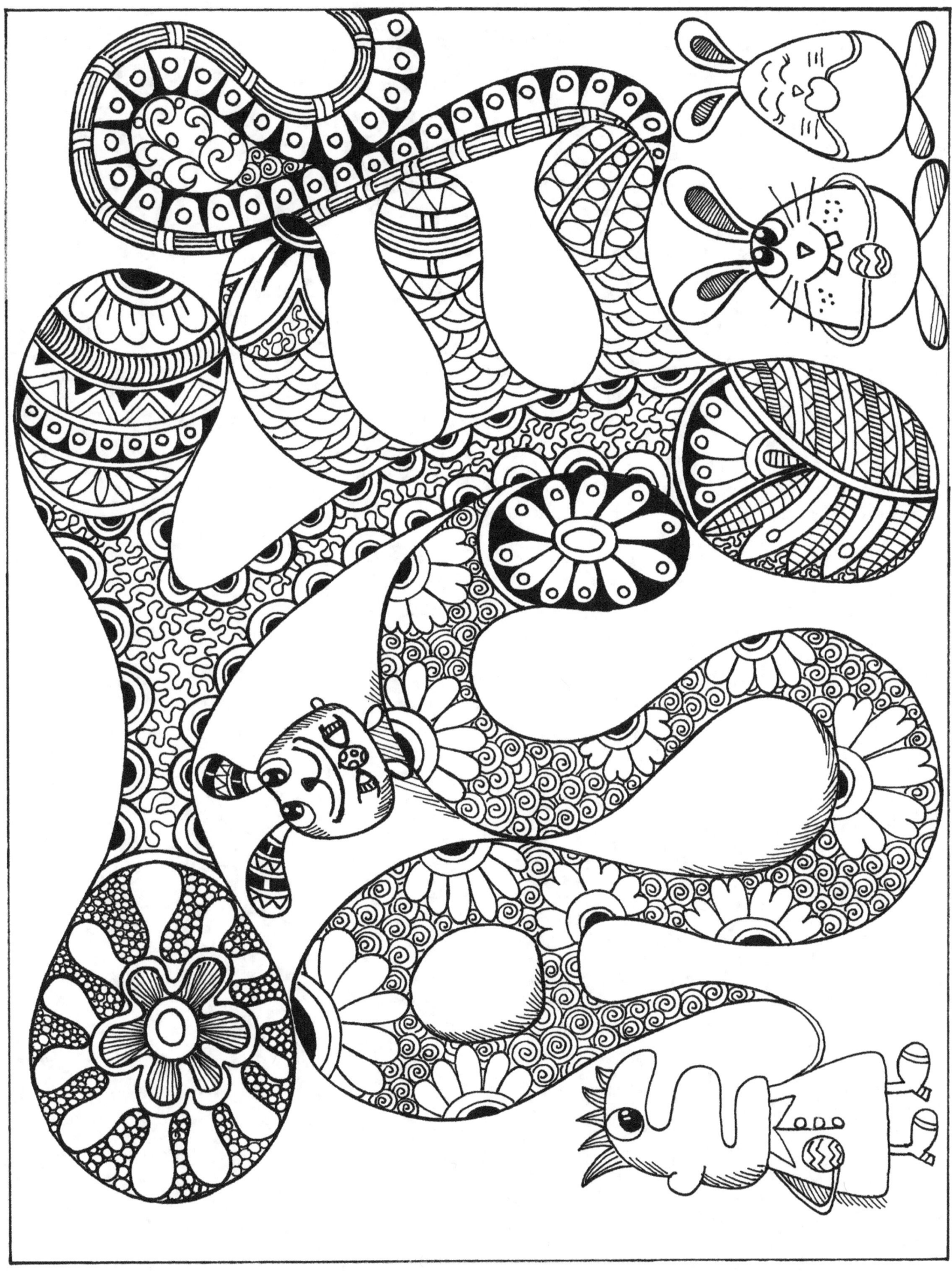

Contributing Artist
Jennifer Rainbow Beryllium
Taiwan

Facebook : DebbieDoodleGarden

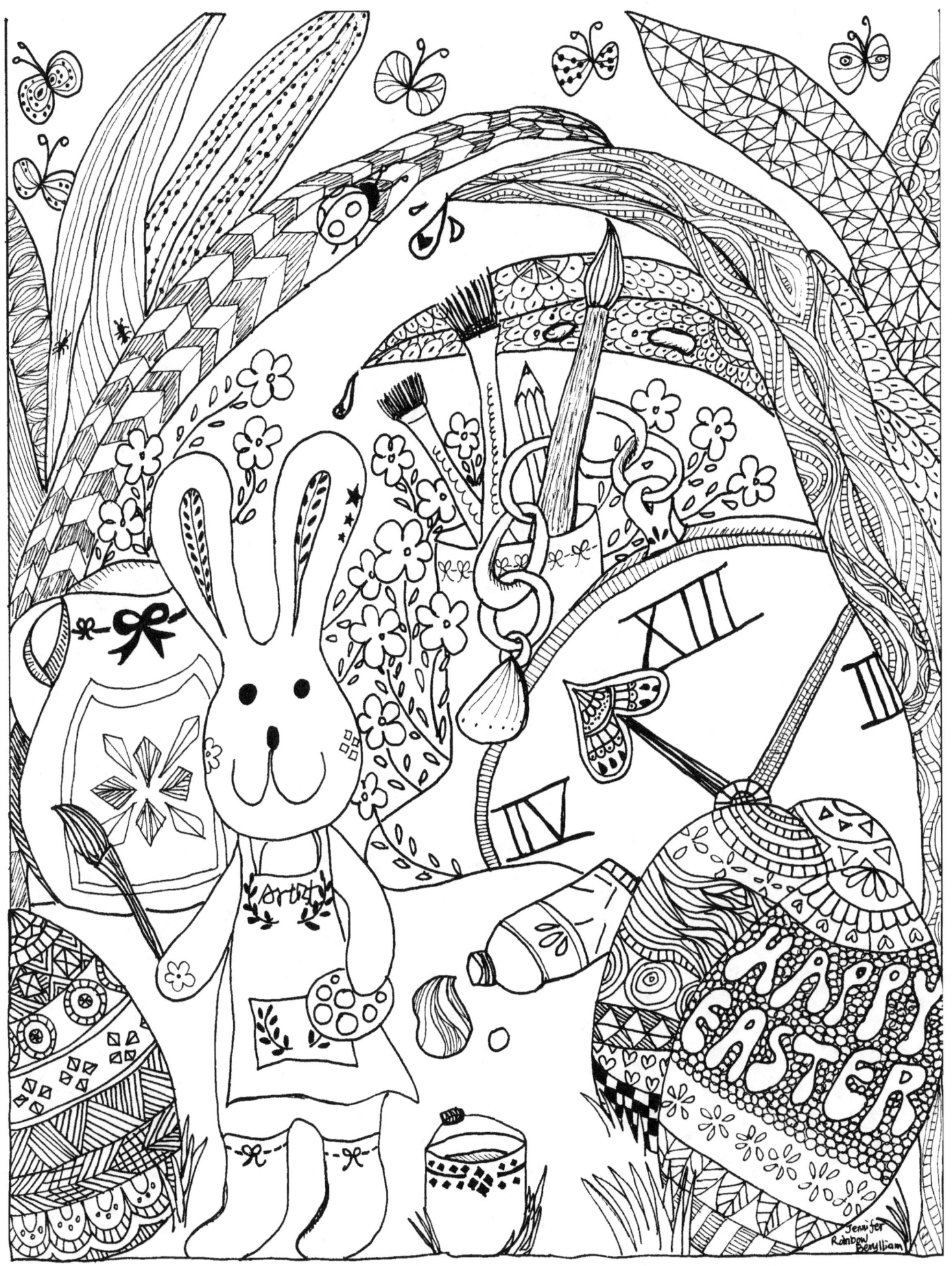

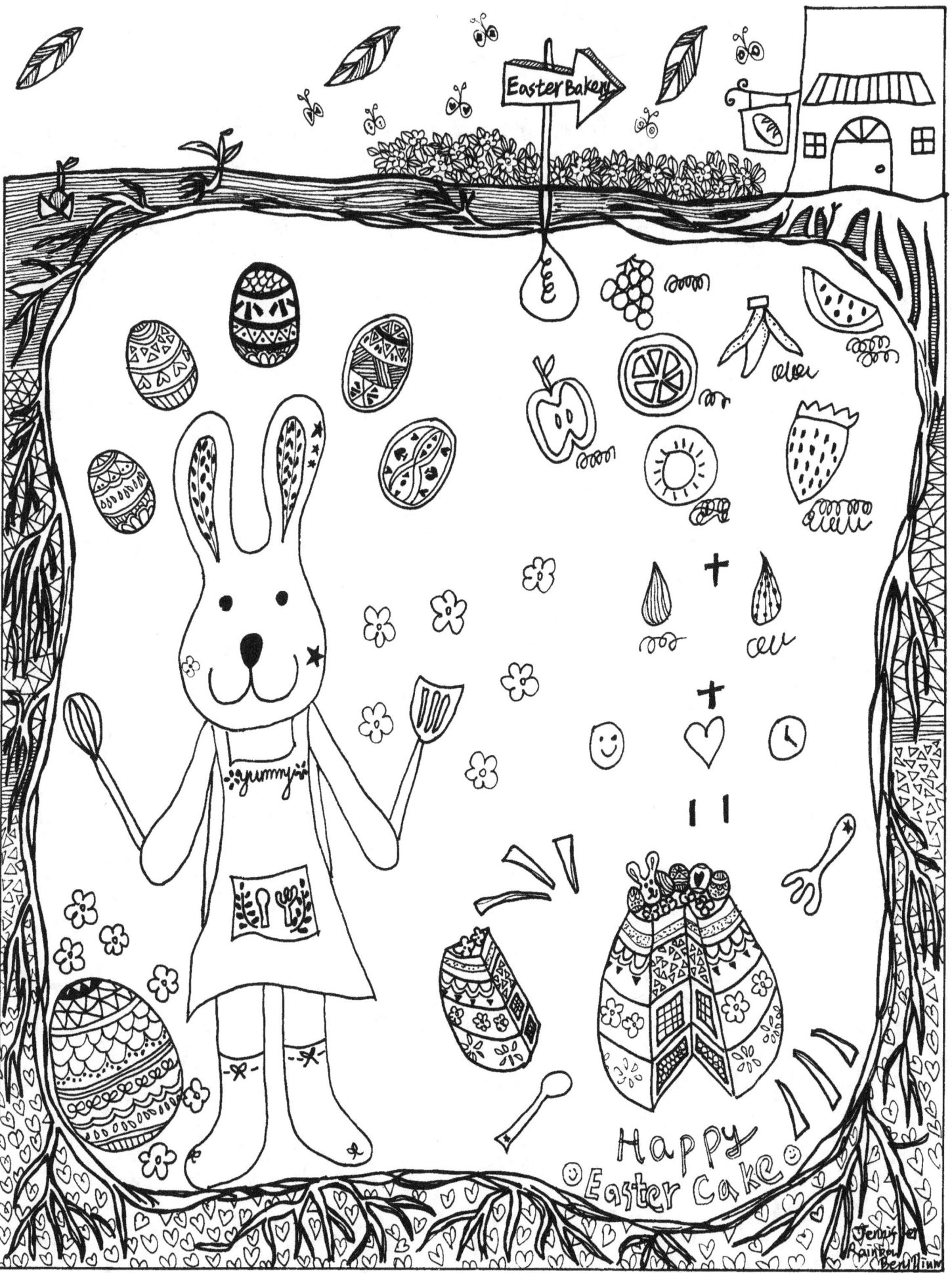

Contributing Artist
Audrey Sagh
Saskatoon, Saskatchewan Canada

Facebook : AMS-Artwork

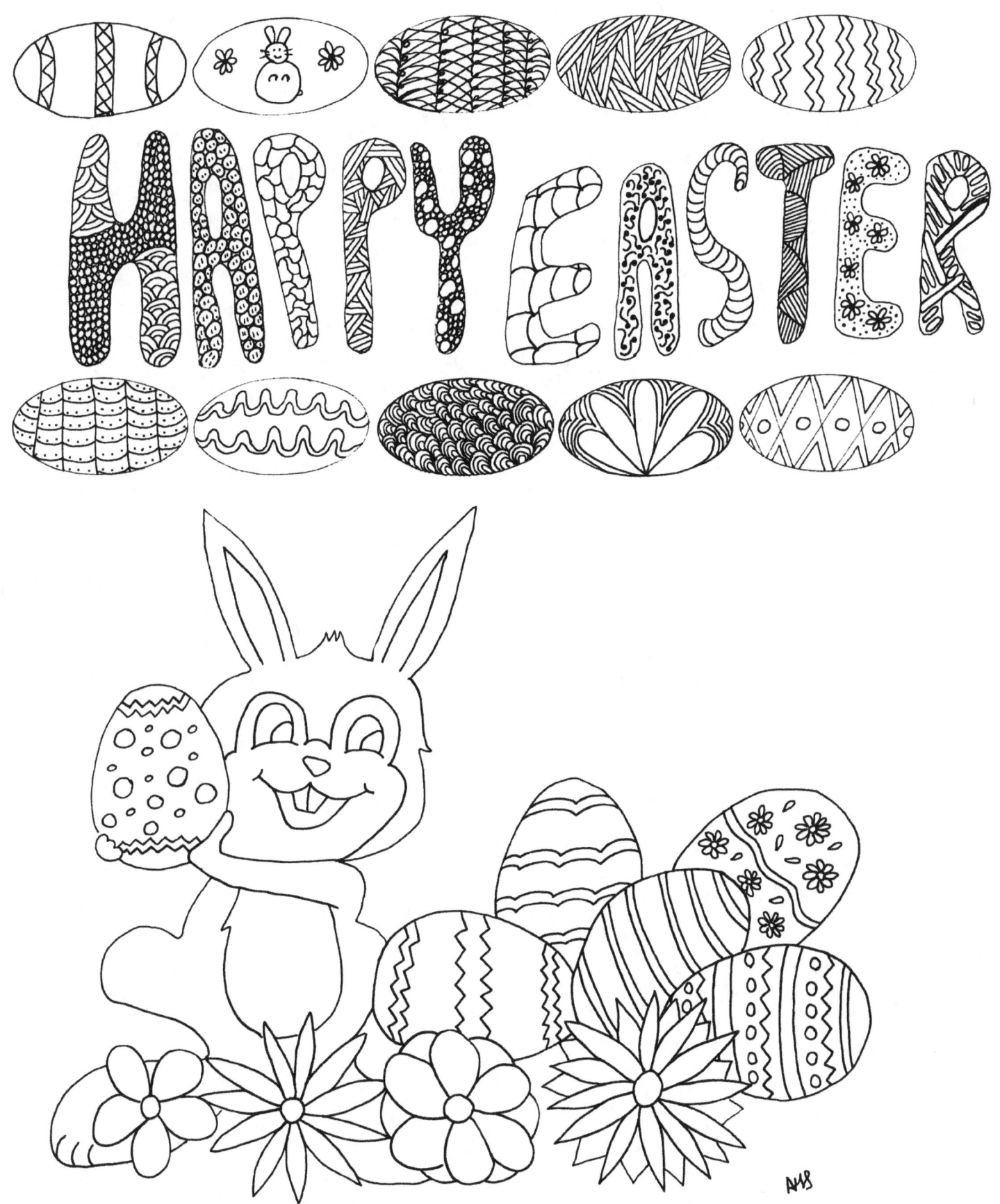

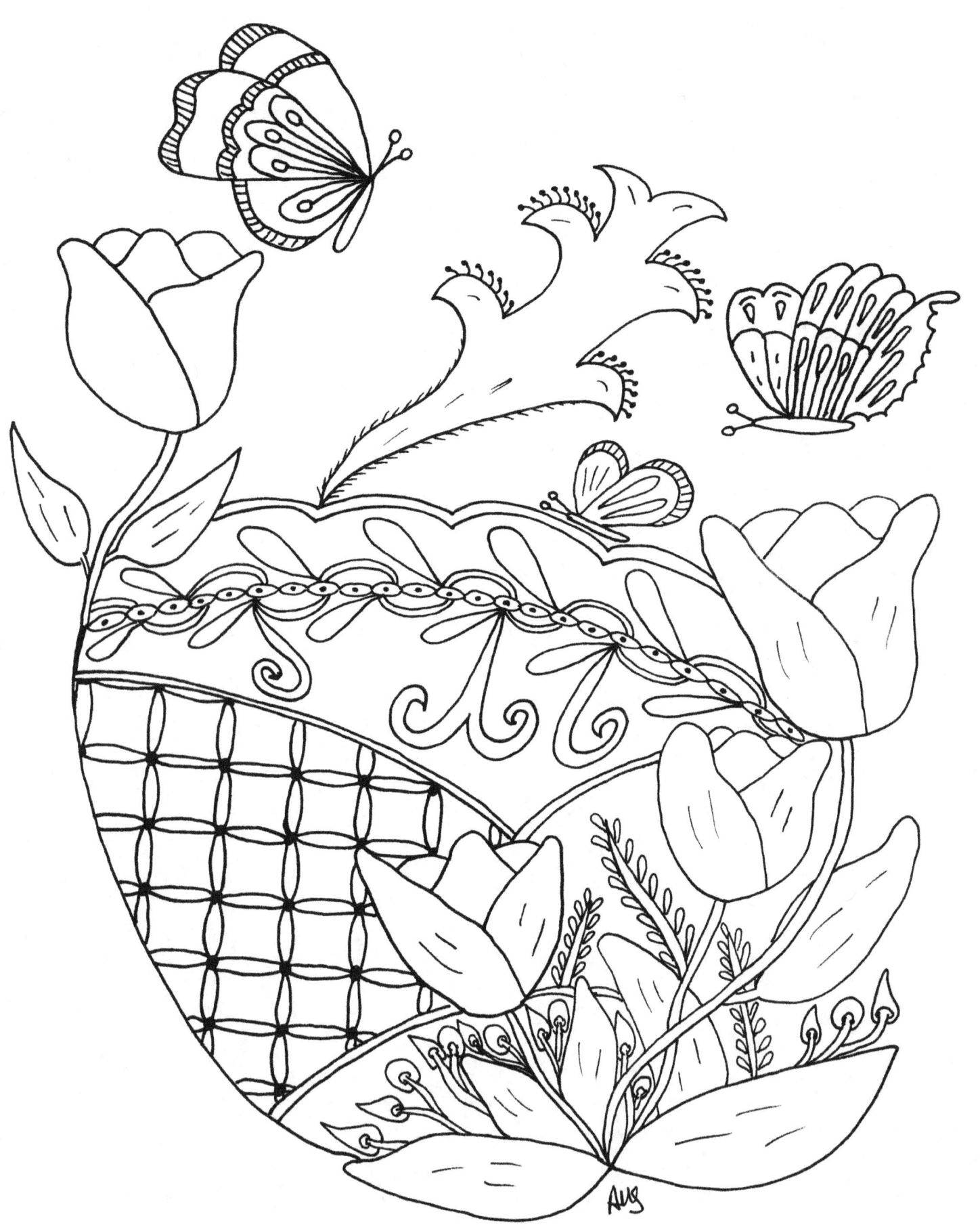

Contributing Artist
Joann Sands
Great Britain

Facebook :JSArt.Strokes

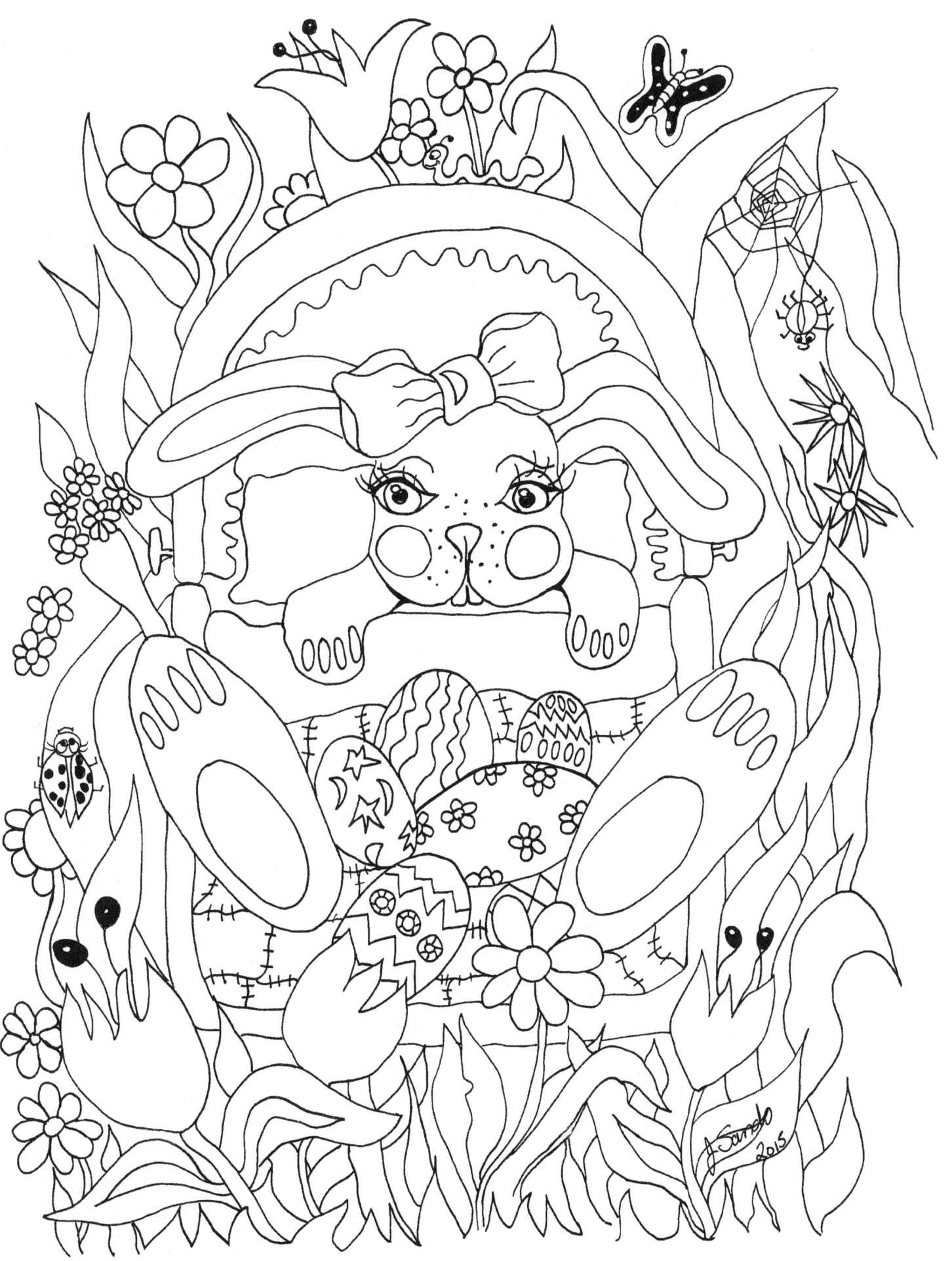

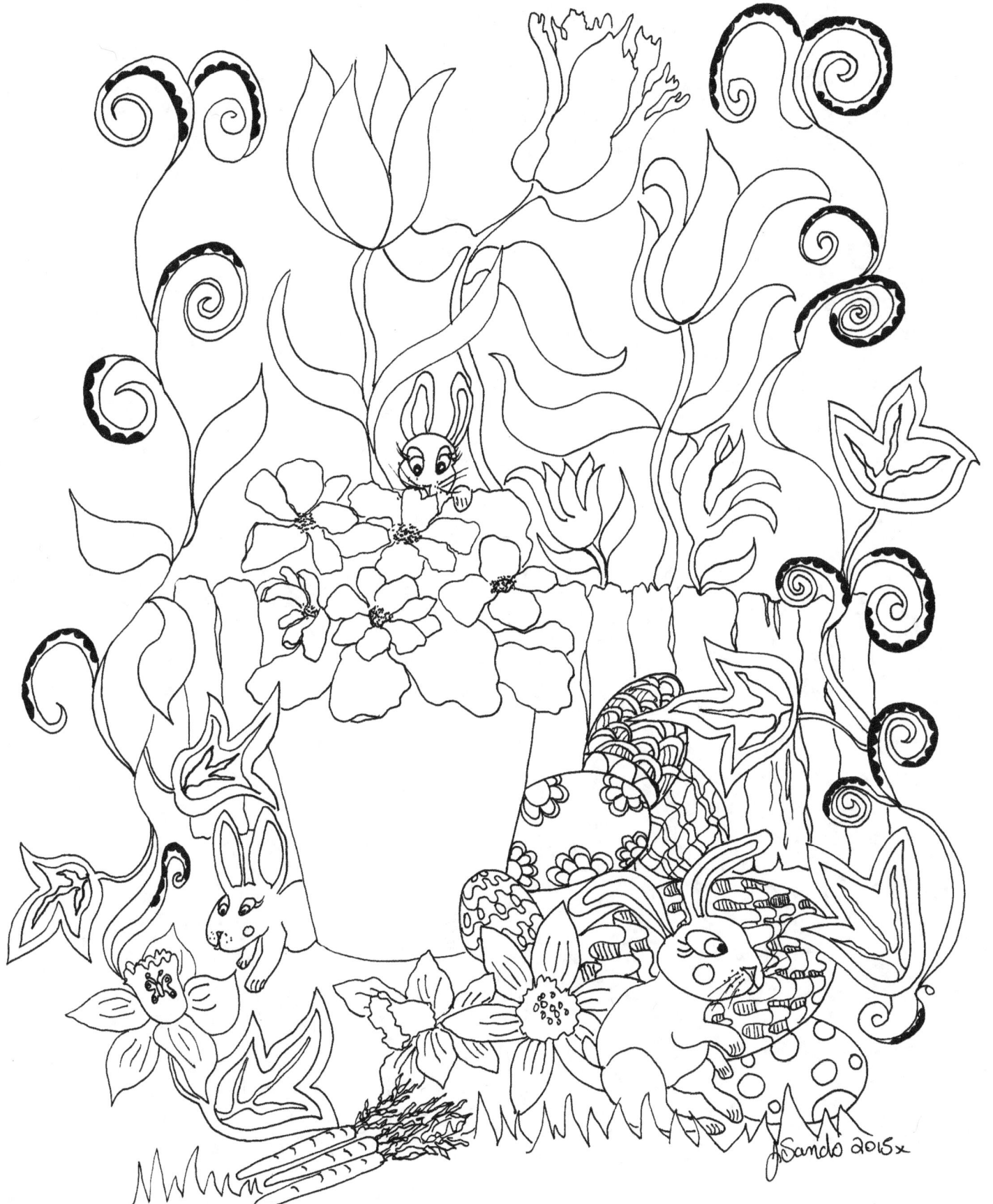

Contributing Artist
Iben Lykke Højholdt
Denmark

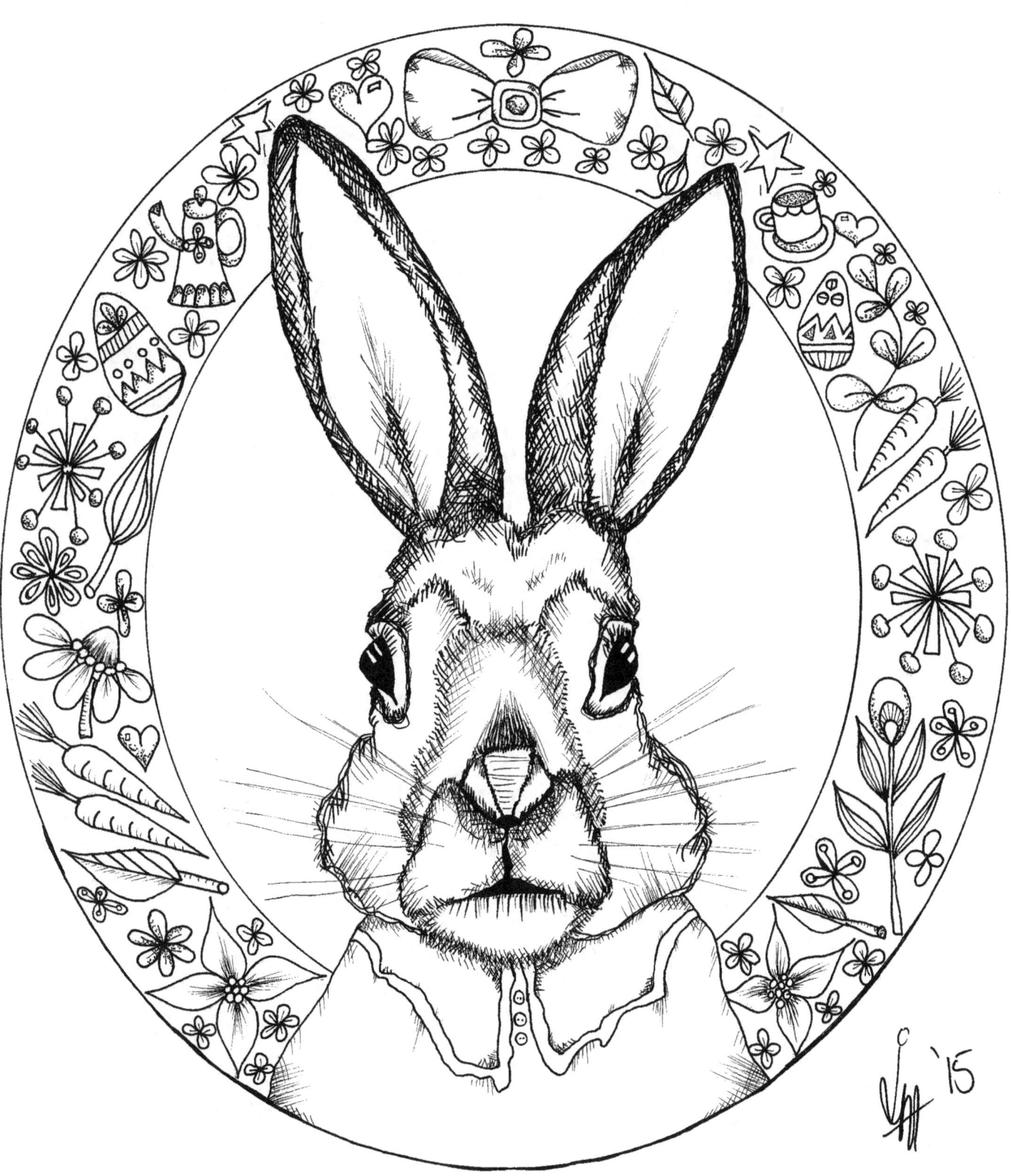

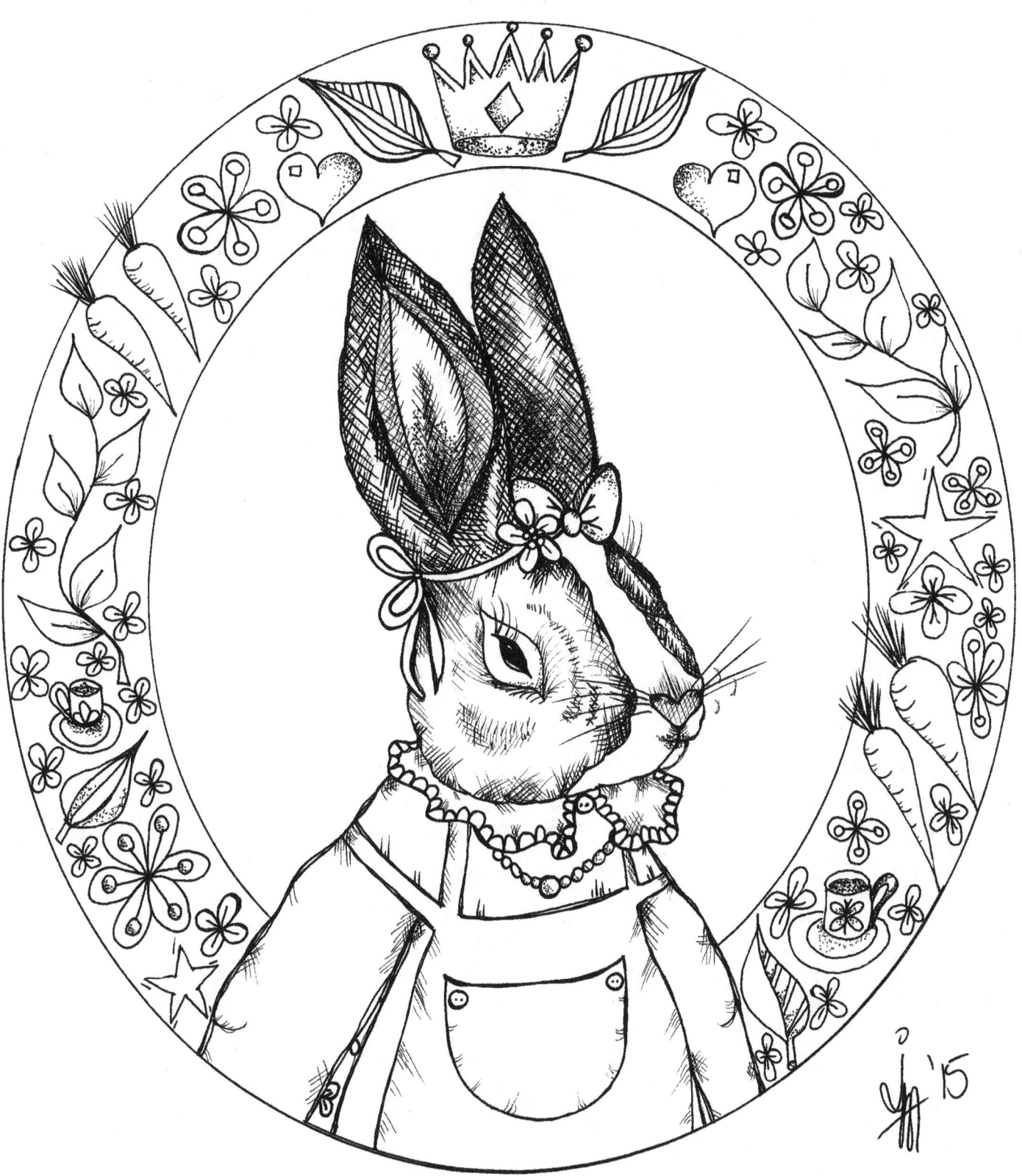

Contributing Artist
Nancy43
Taiwan

Facebook : 43Nancy43

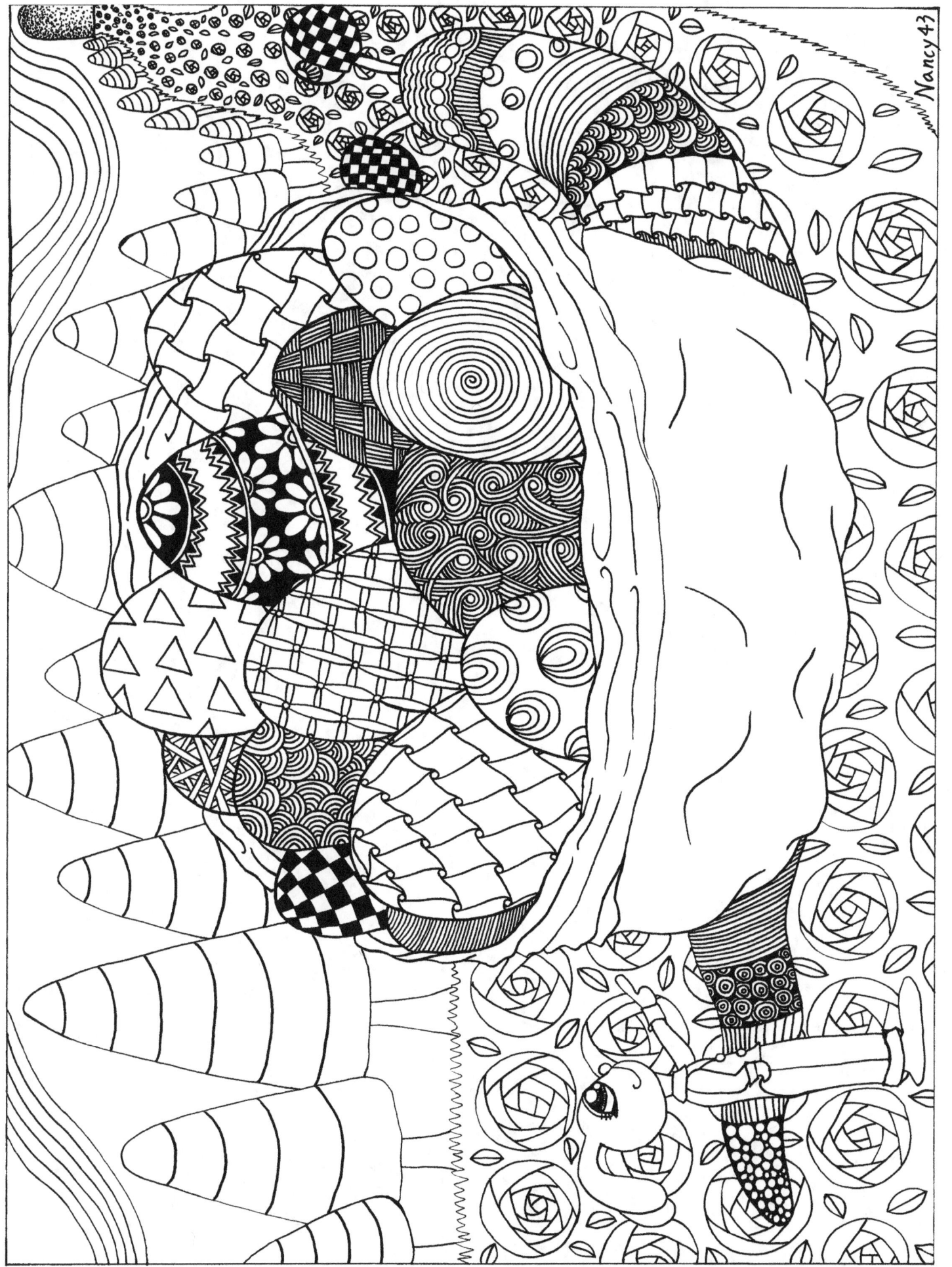

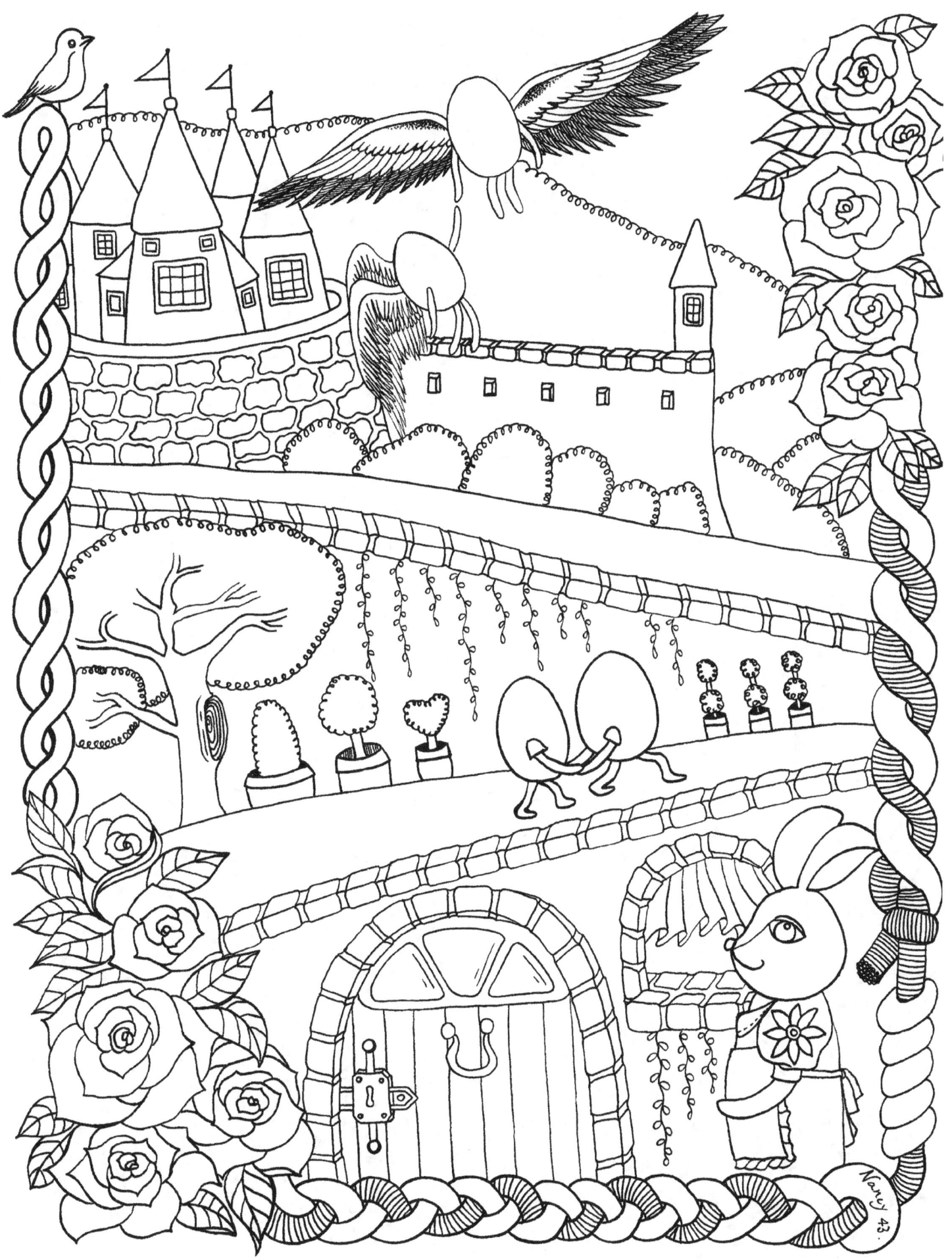

Contributing Artist
L'aety Esperanza
France

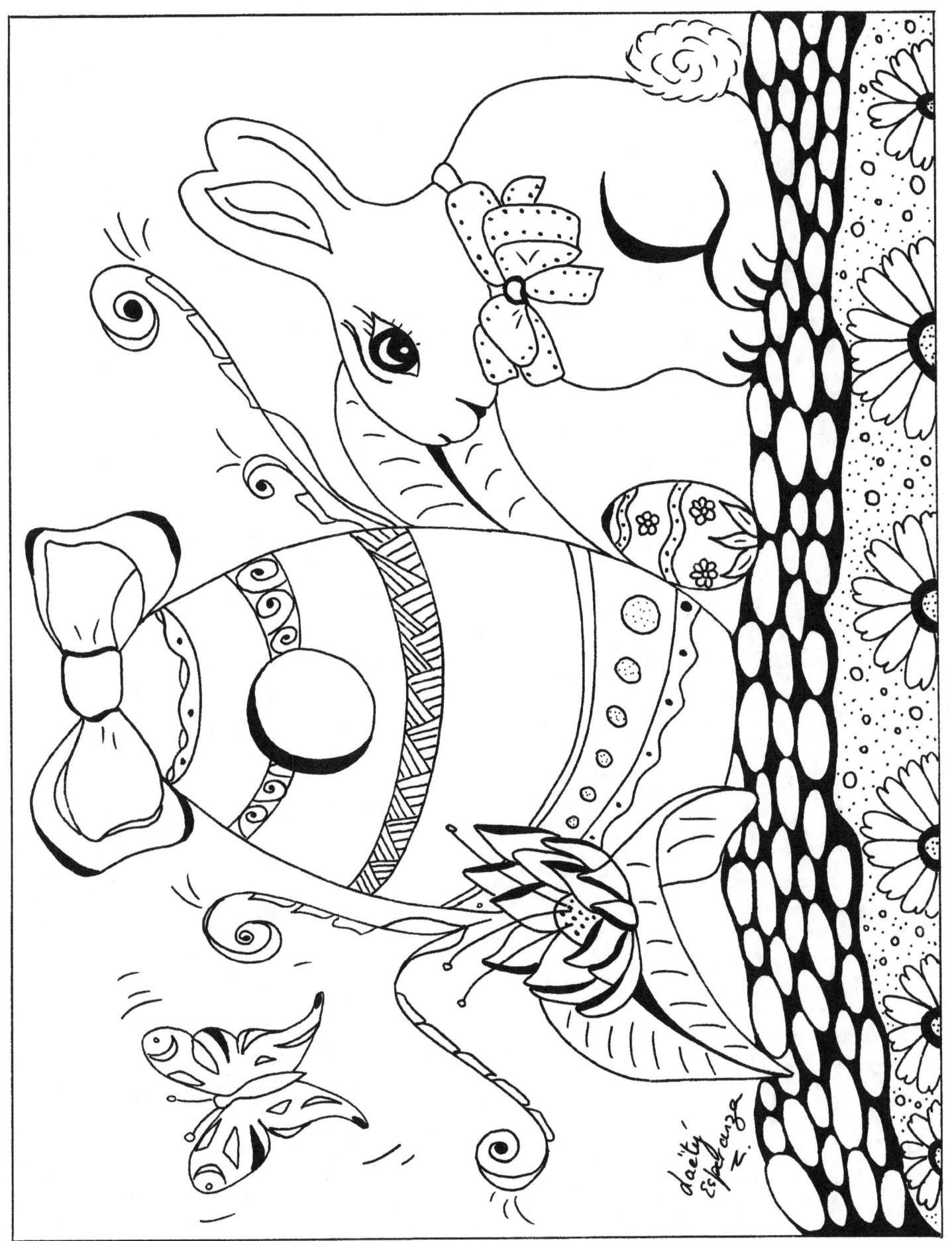

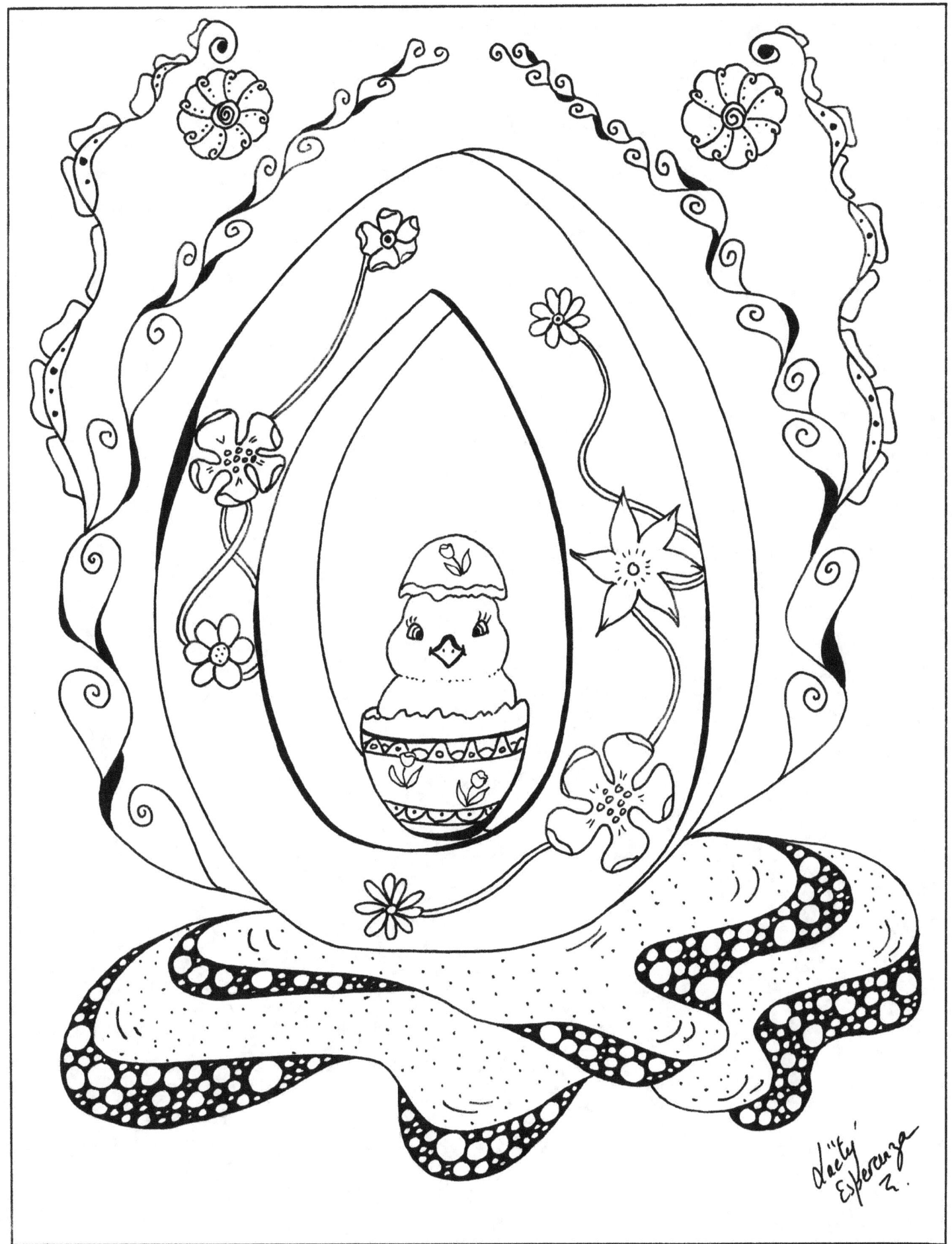

Contributing Artist
Debbie Lai
Taiwan

Facebook : DebbieDoodleGarden

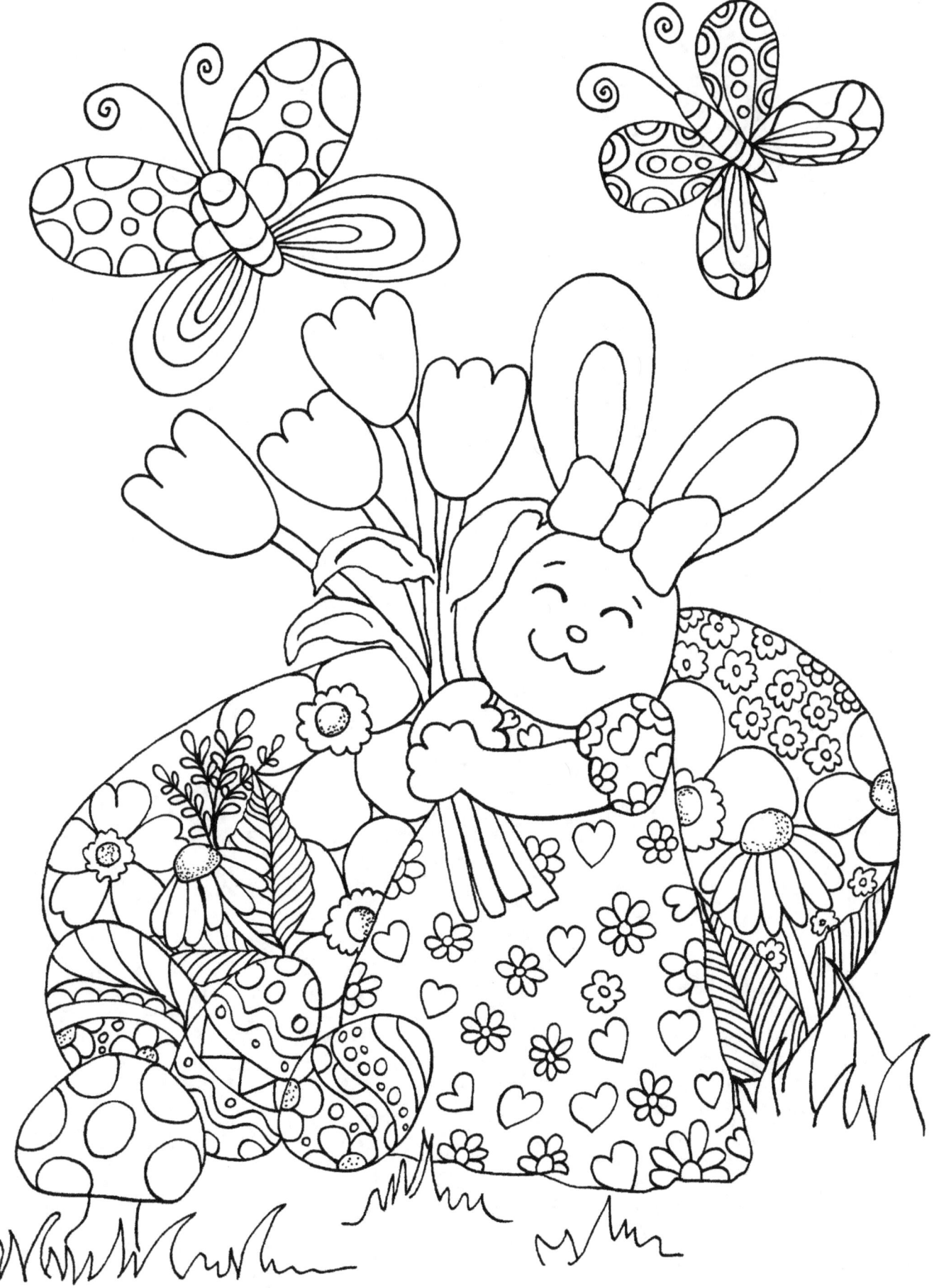

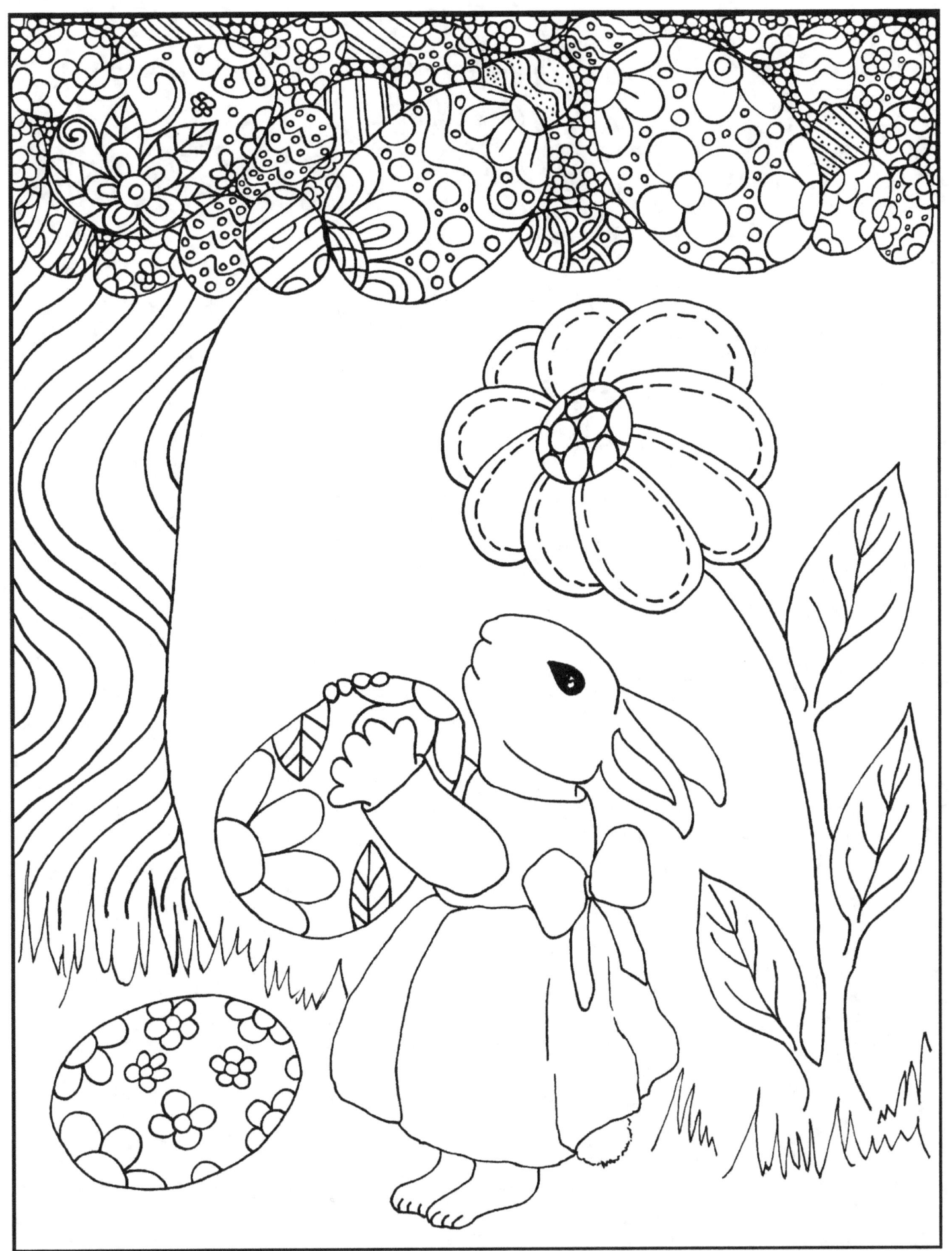

Contributing Artist
Neeti Goswami
Canada

www.artbyneeti.ca

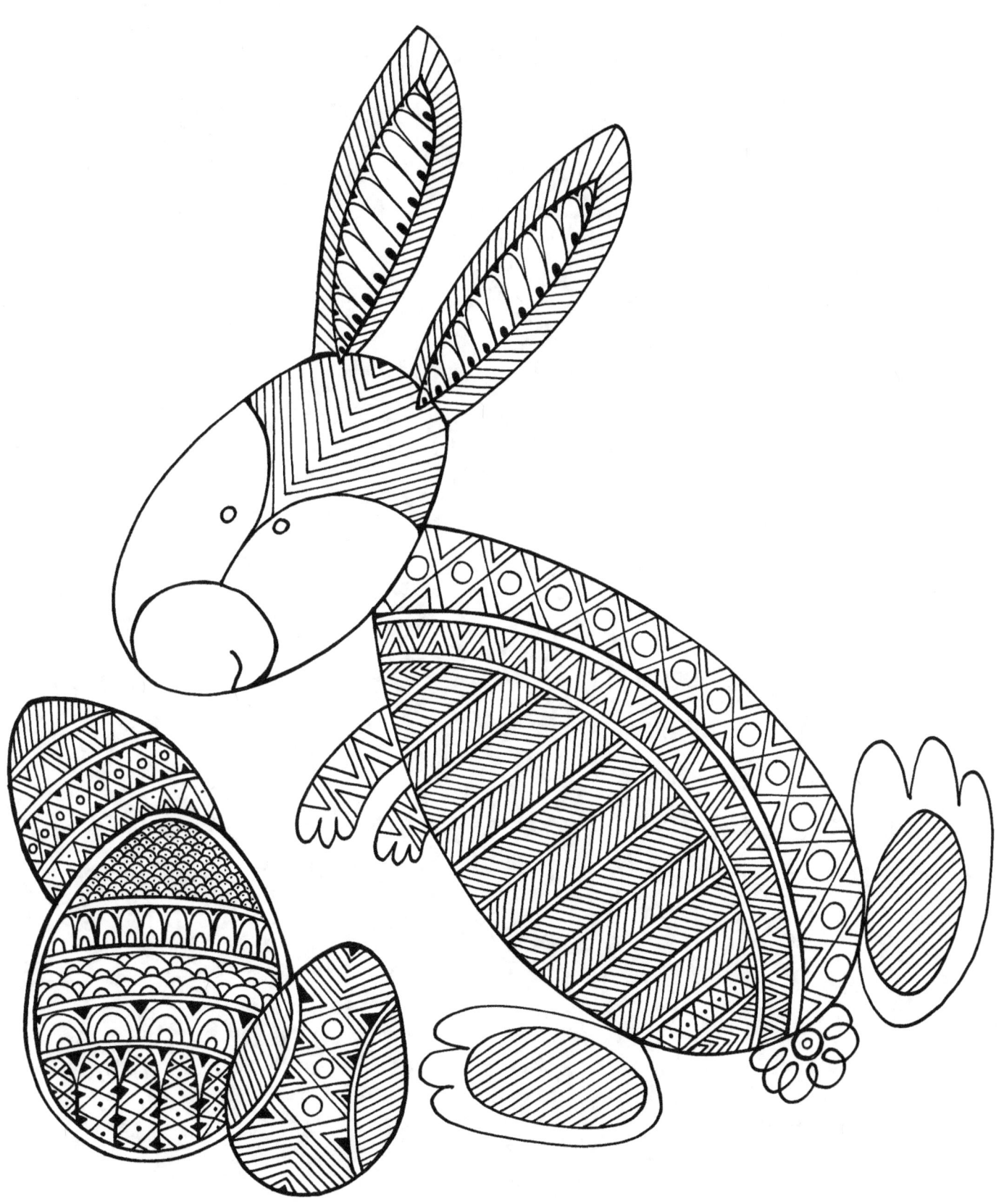

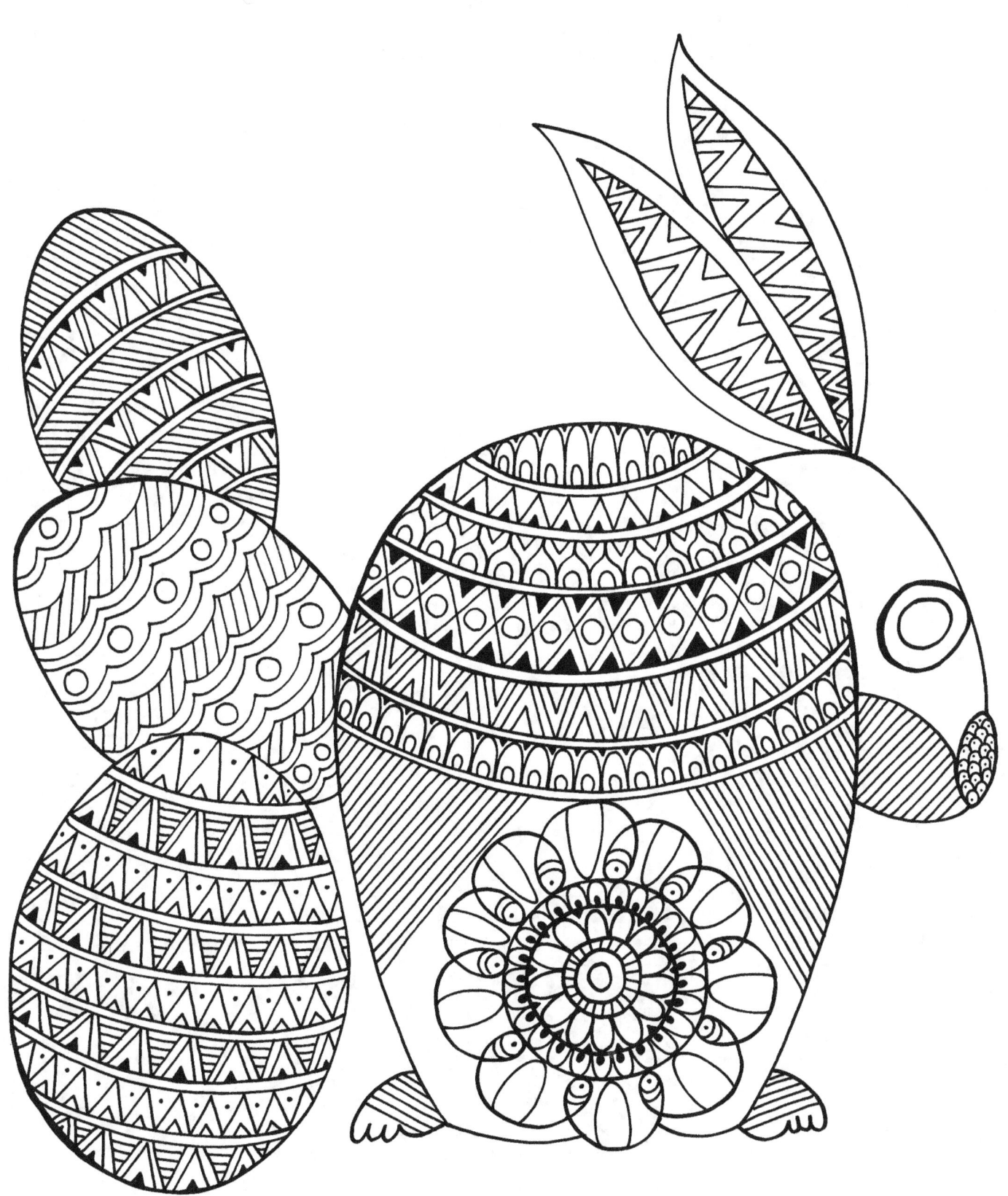

Contributing Artist
Maud Feral Chauveau
(MFC)
France

« MFC - Peinture, graphisme & illustration »

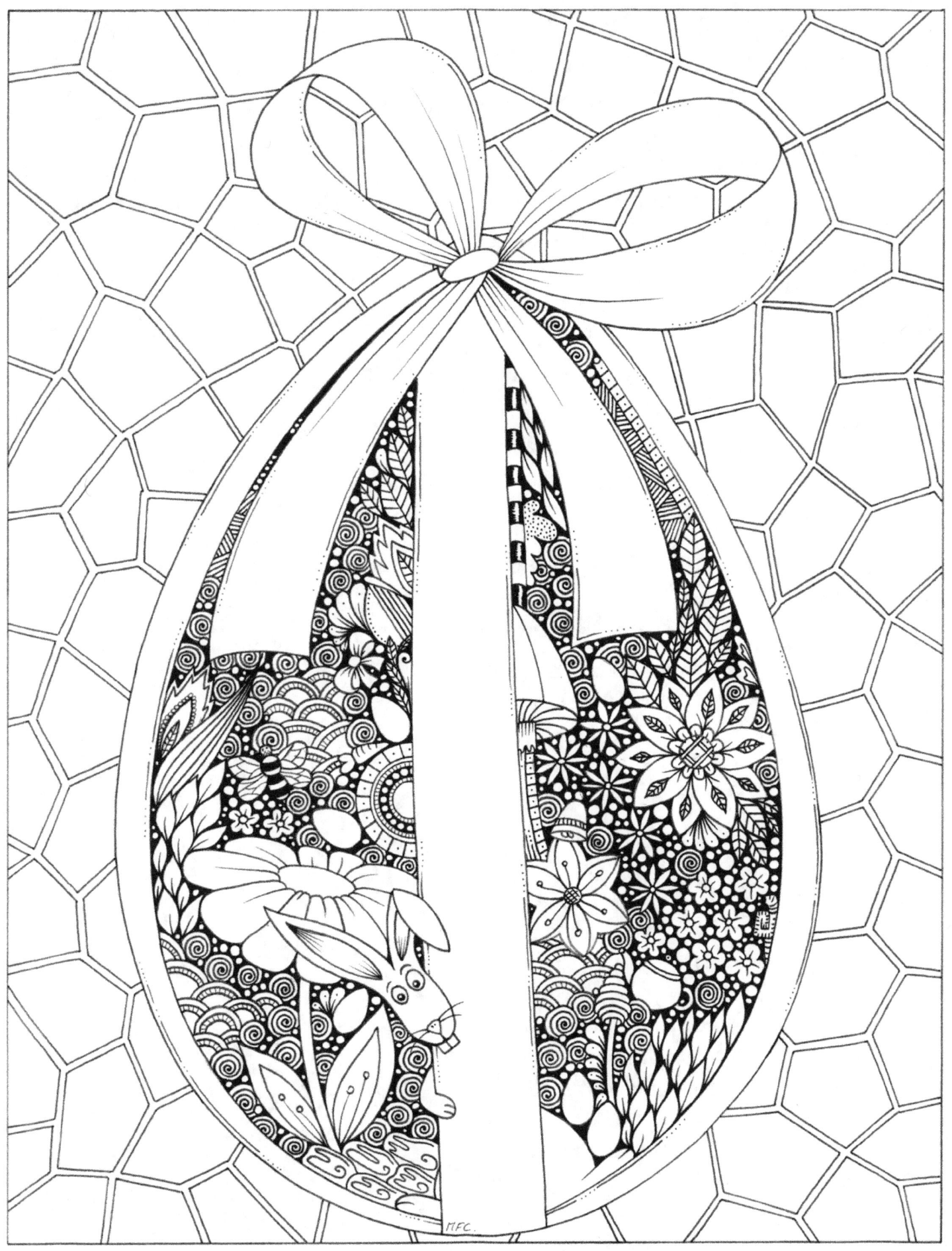

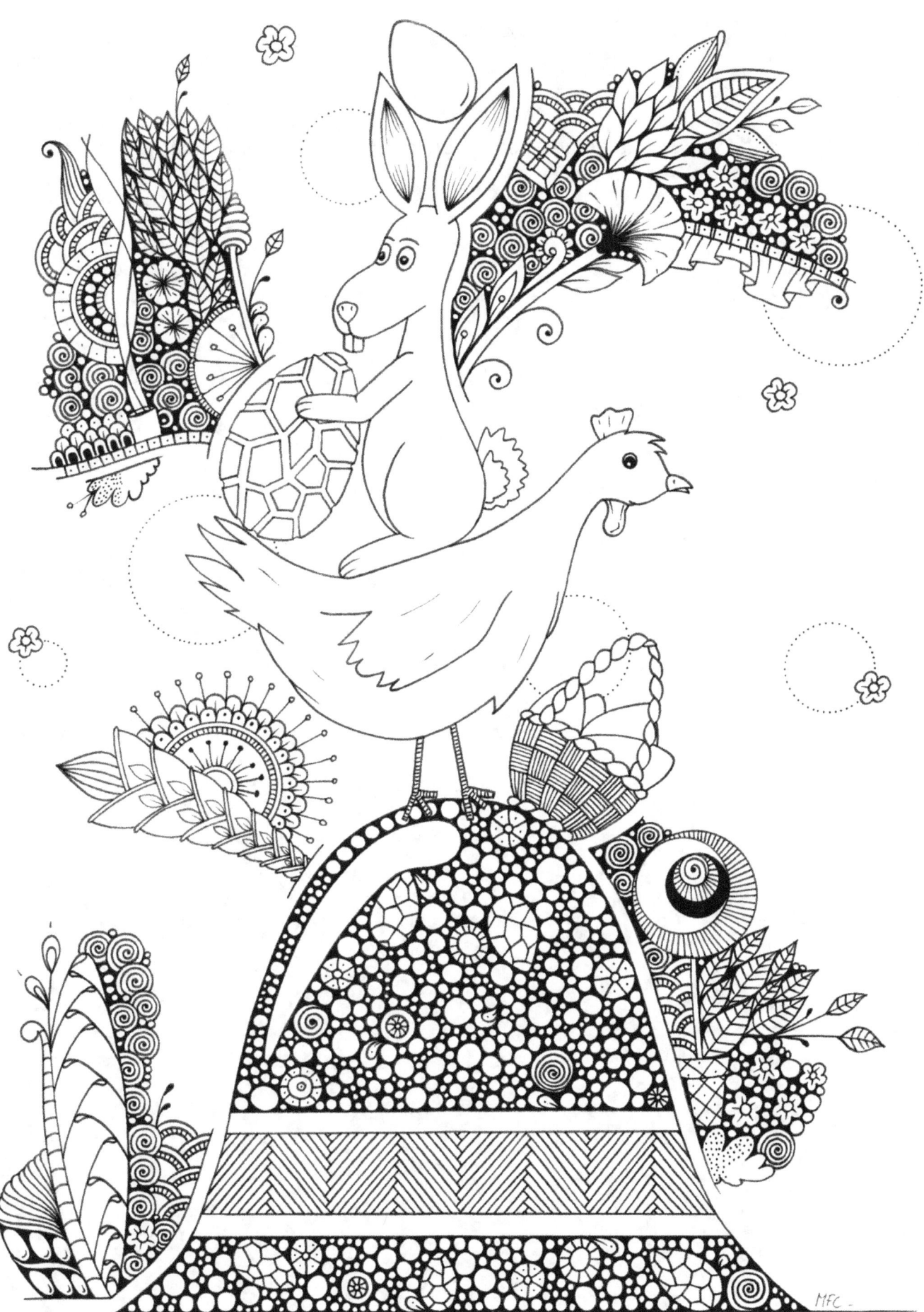

Contributing Artist
Orbleue's
France

http://www.alittlemarket.com/boutique/orbleue-1682885.html

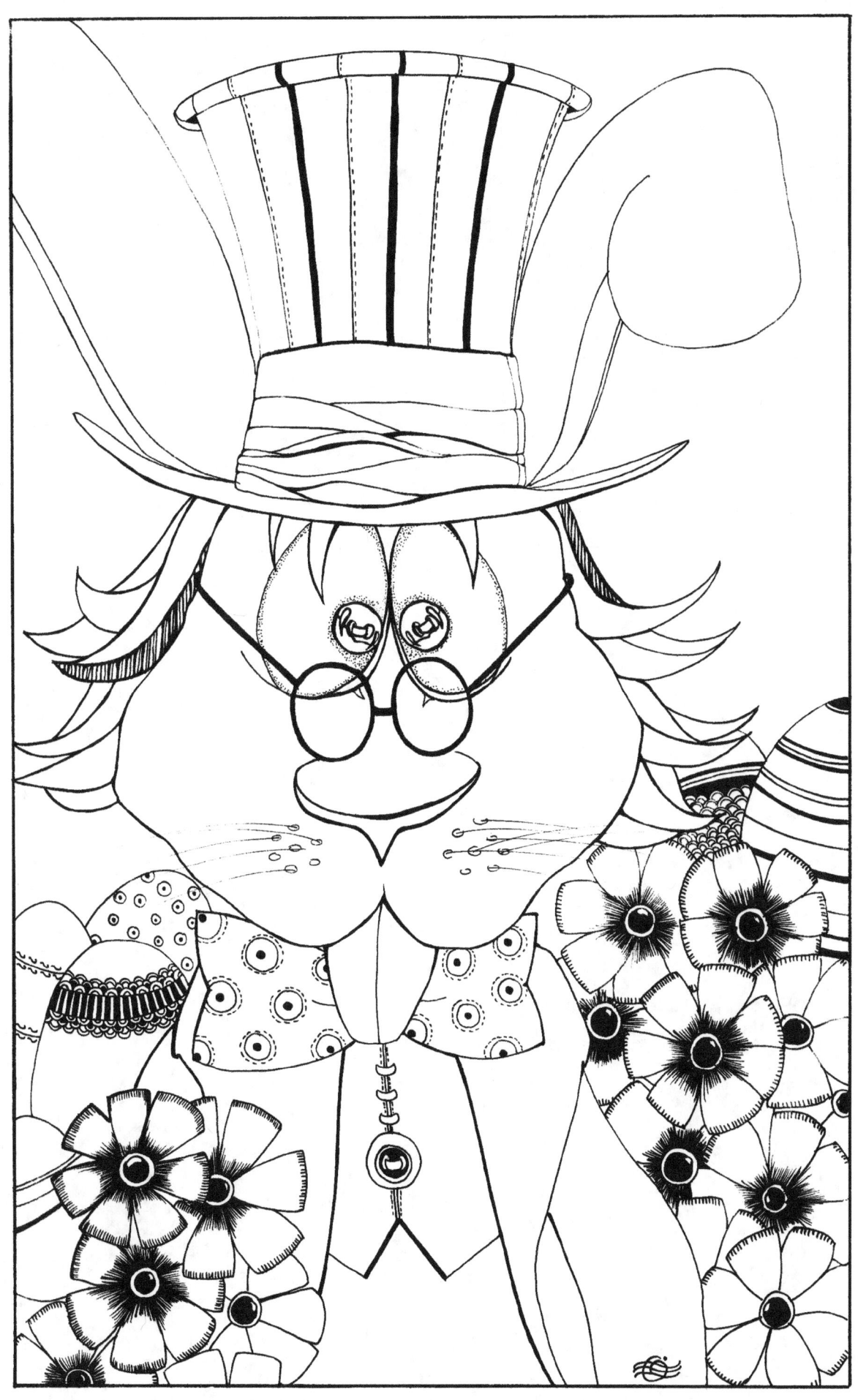

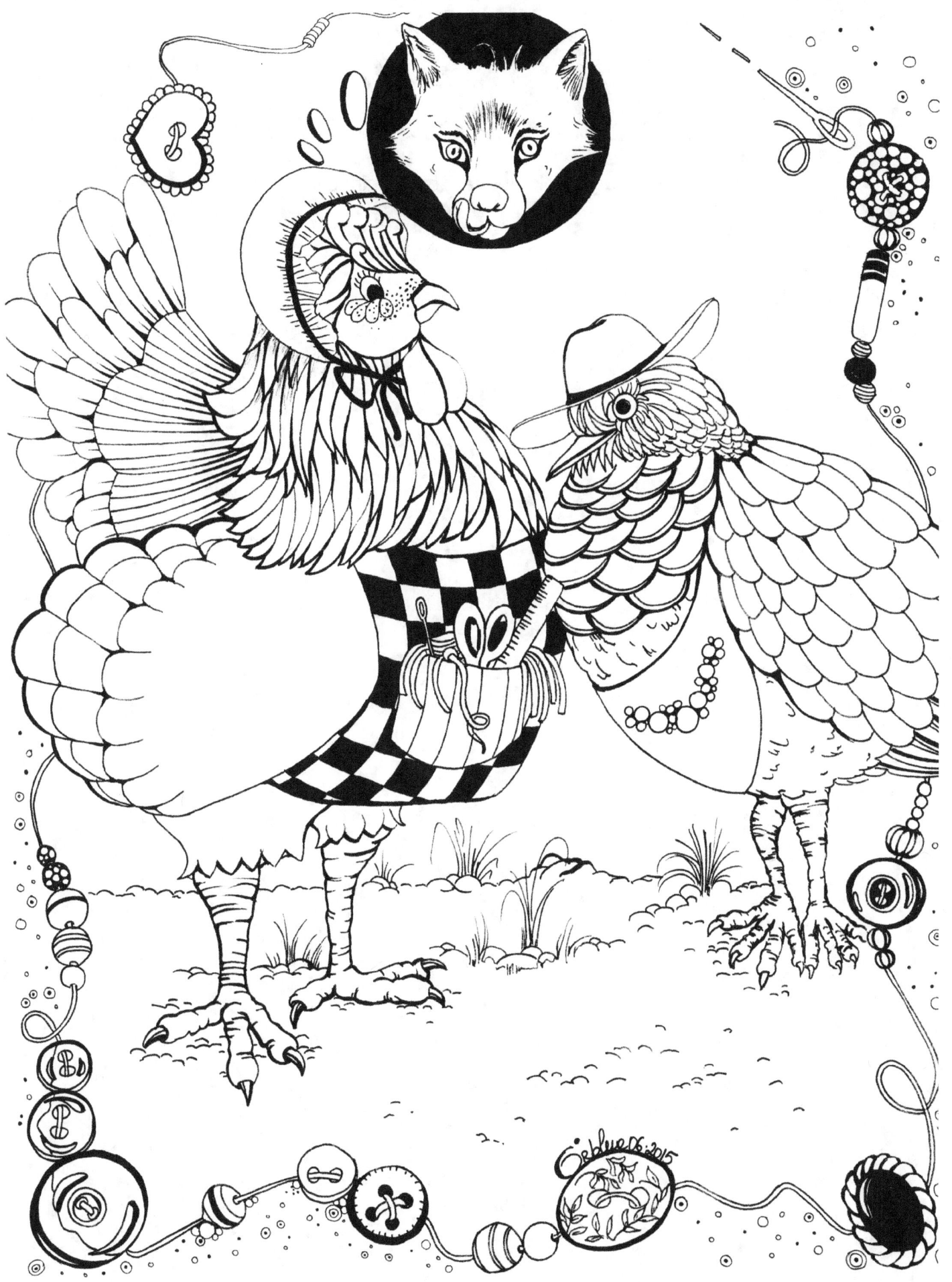

Contributing Artist
Marie-Eve Klein
Belgium
Facebook : lestraitsorsdemimieve

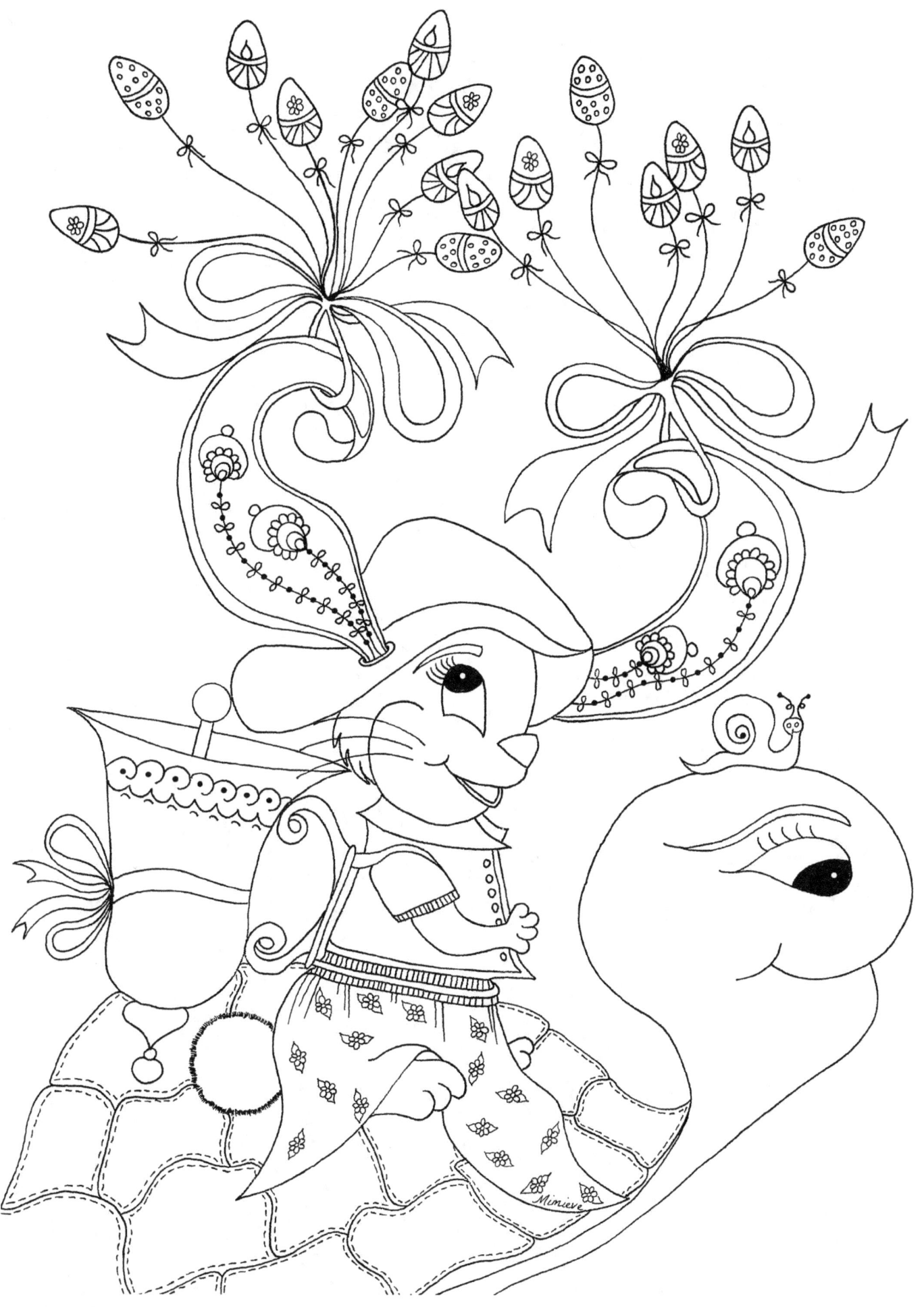

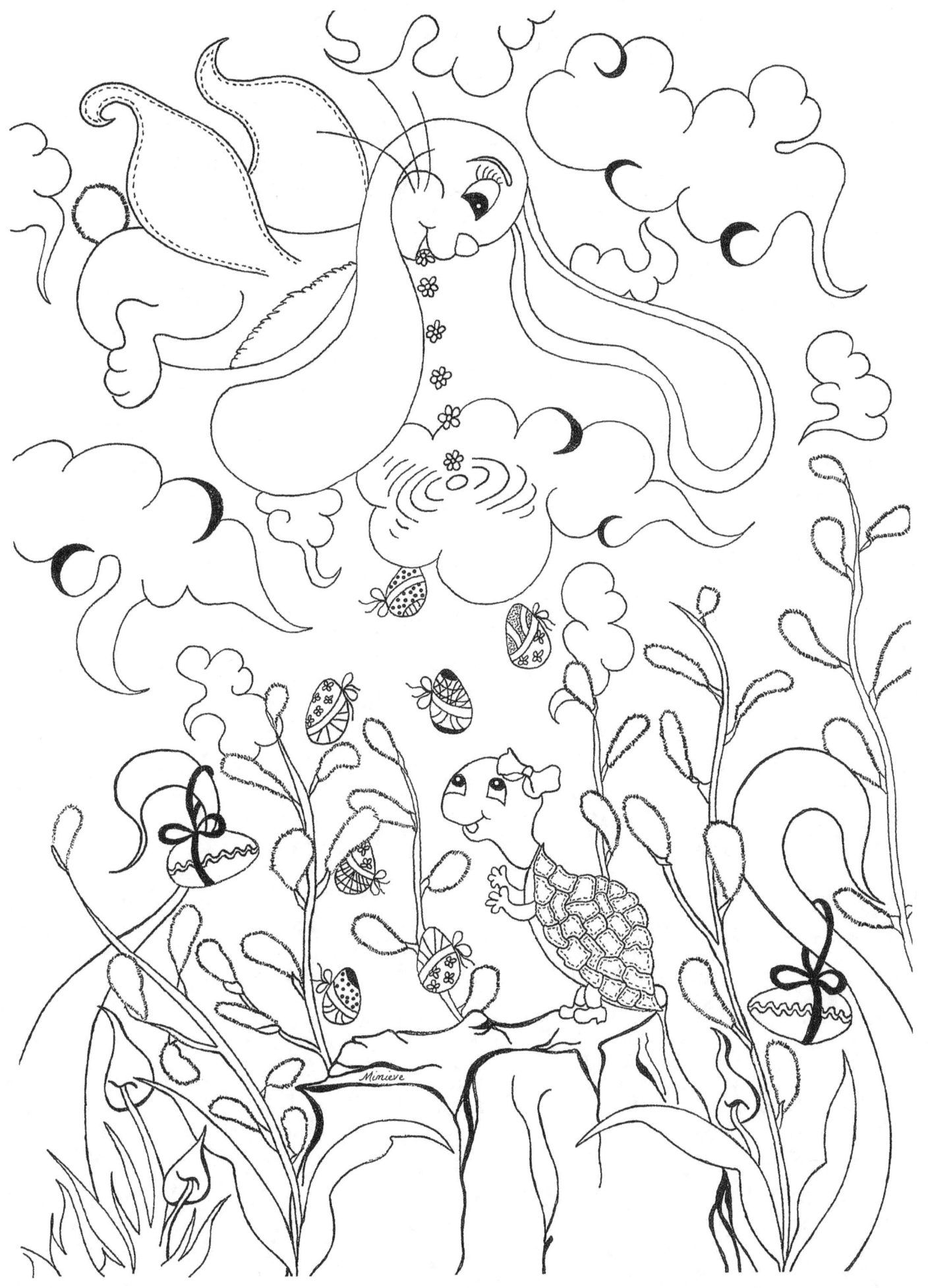

Contributing Artist
Mireille Westerduin, Colour by Mi
The Netherlands

Facebook : Colour-by-Mi-Kleurplaten-Illustraties

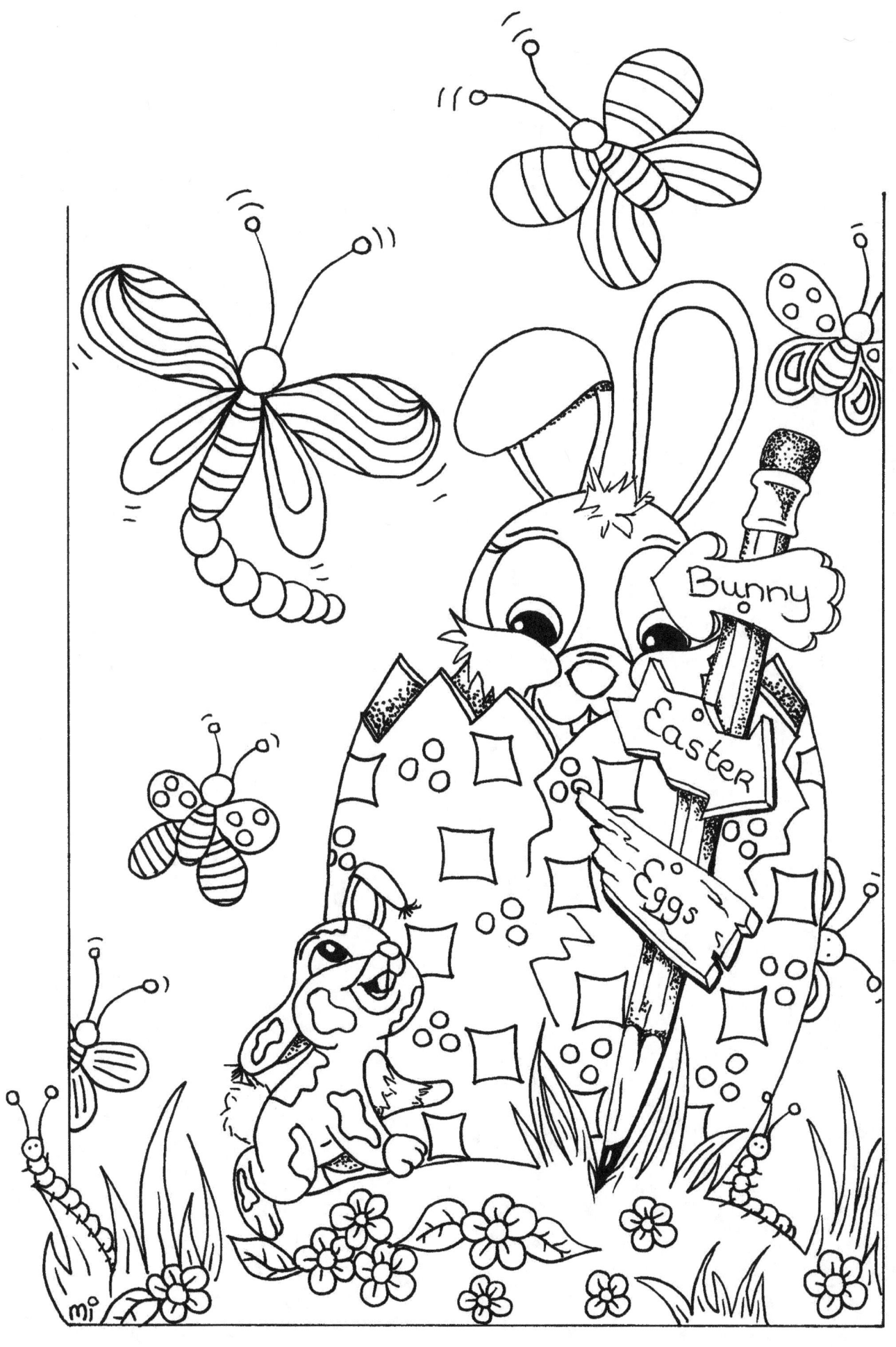

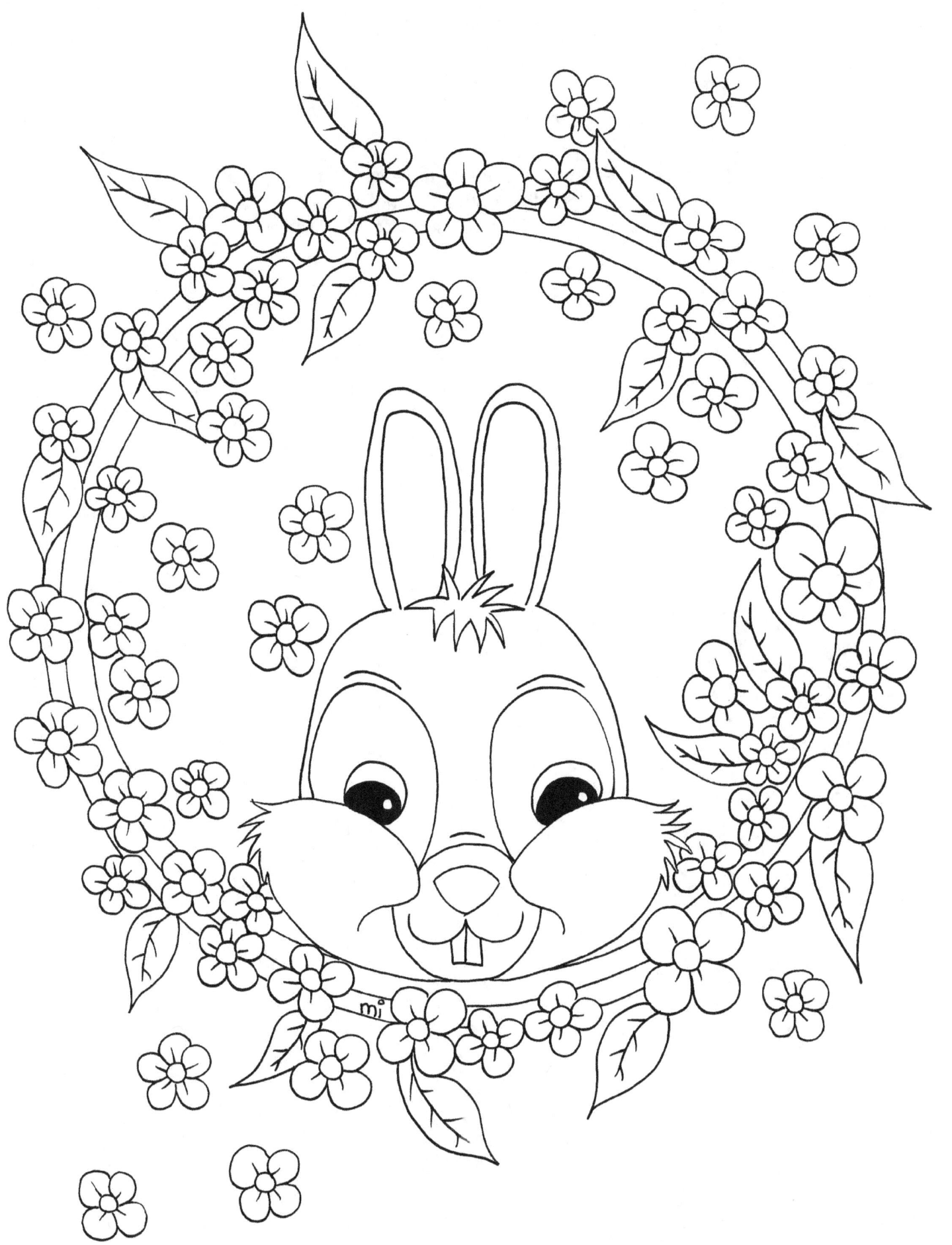

Contributing Artist
Ellen Wolters
The Netherlands

http://www.tekenpraktijkdeinnerlijkewereld.blogspot.nl/
http://ellenstraties.blogspot.nl/
https://www.youtube.com/user/DIWEllenWolters

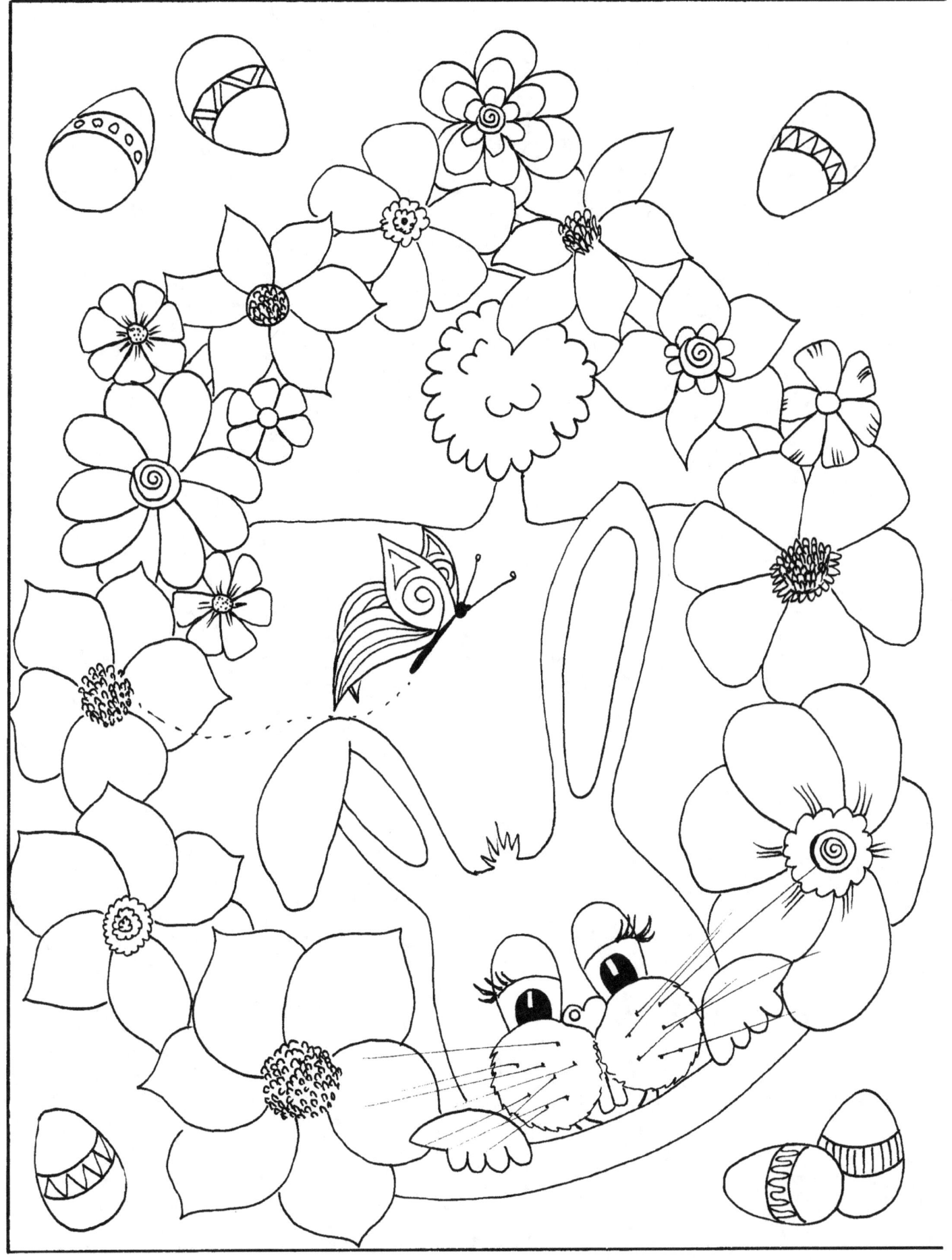

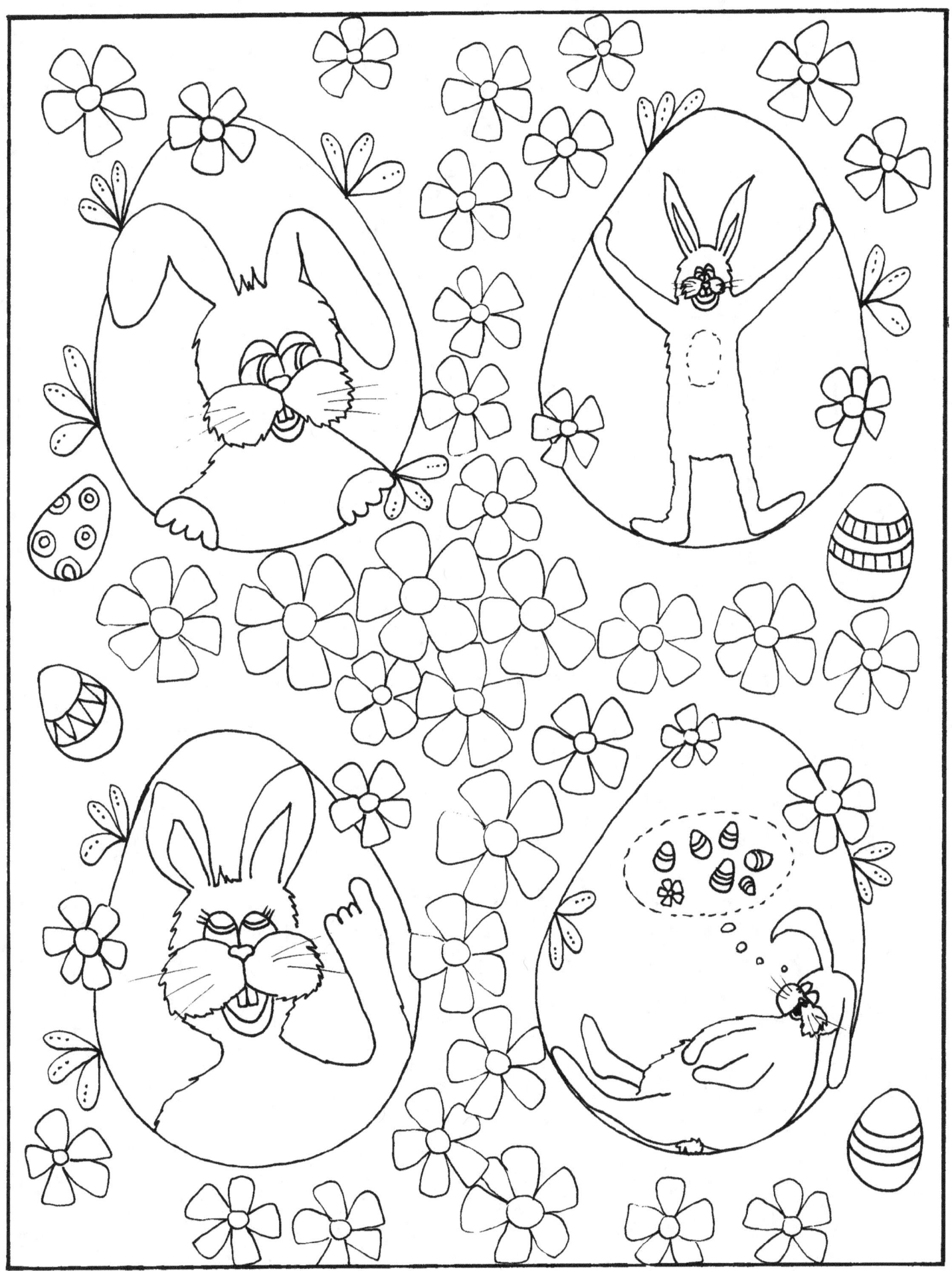

Contributing Artist
Ondine Summers
U.K.

Facebook : ColourIt

Etsy shop : colouritbooks

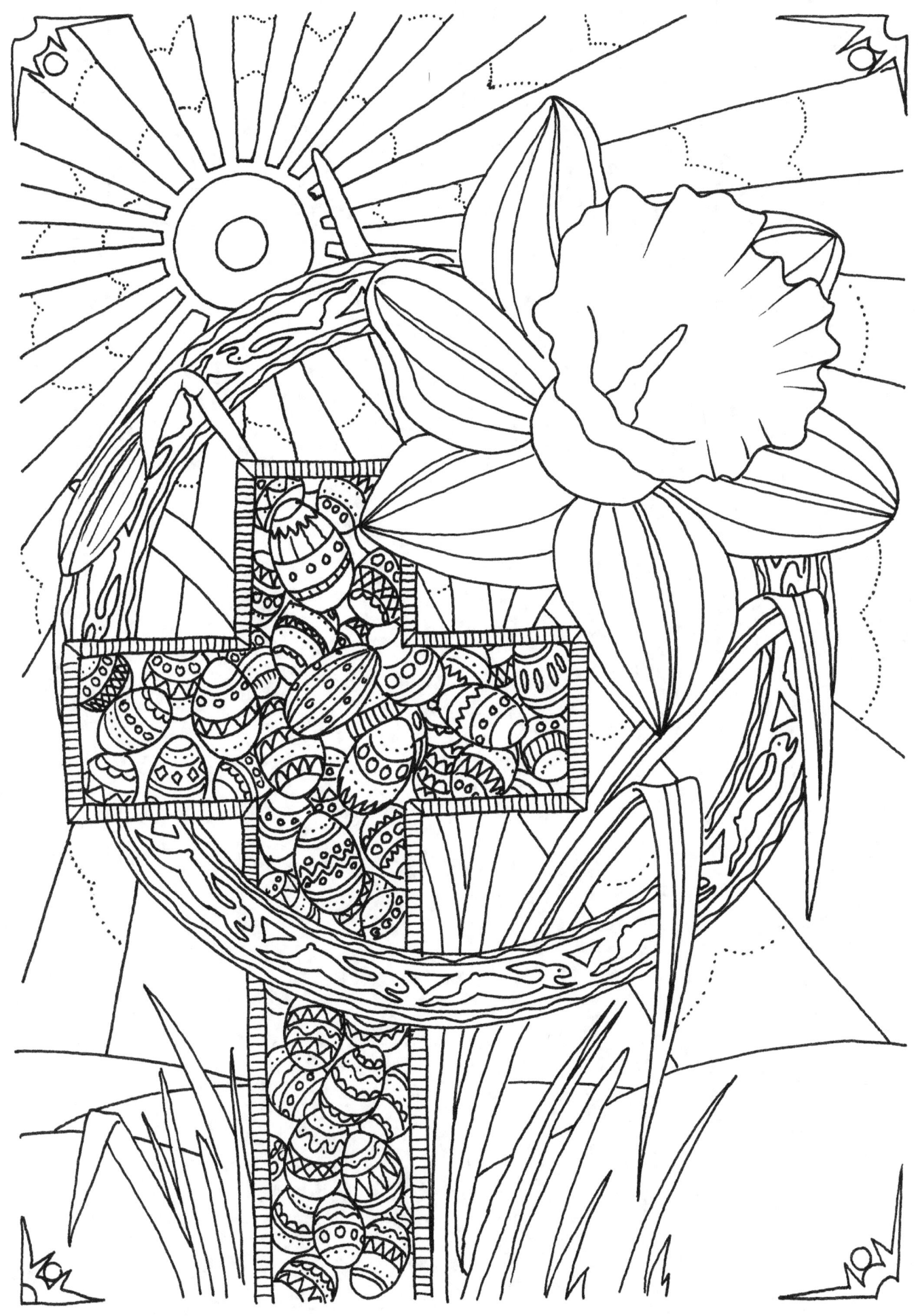

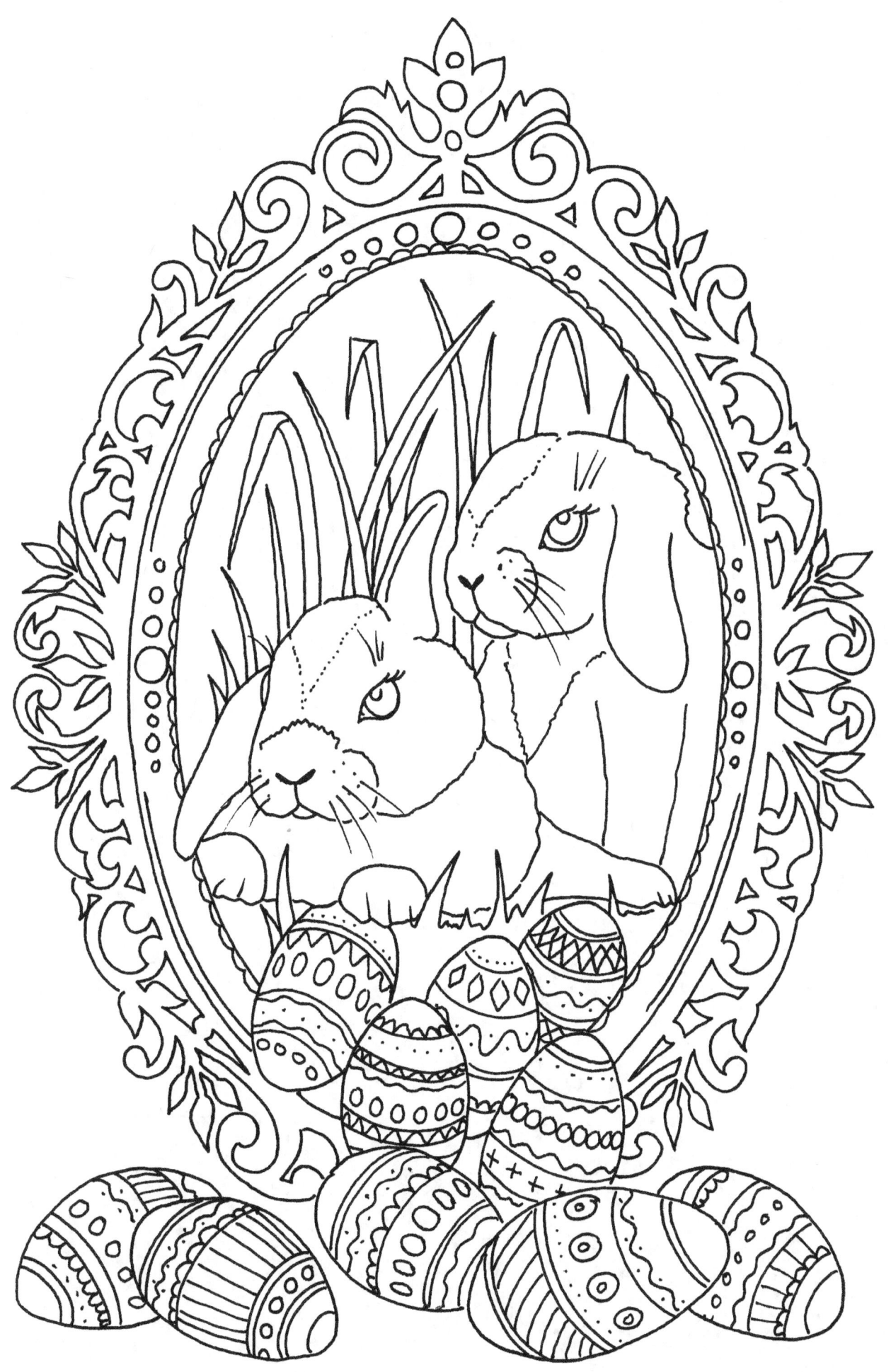

Contributing Artist
Peggy Sue's Artwork
The Netherlands

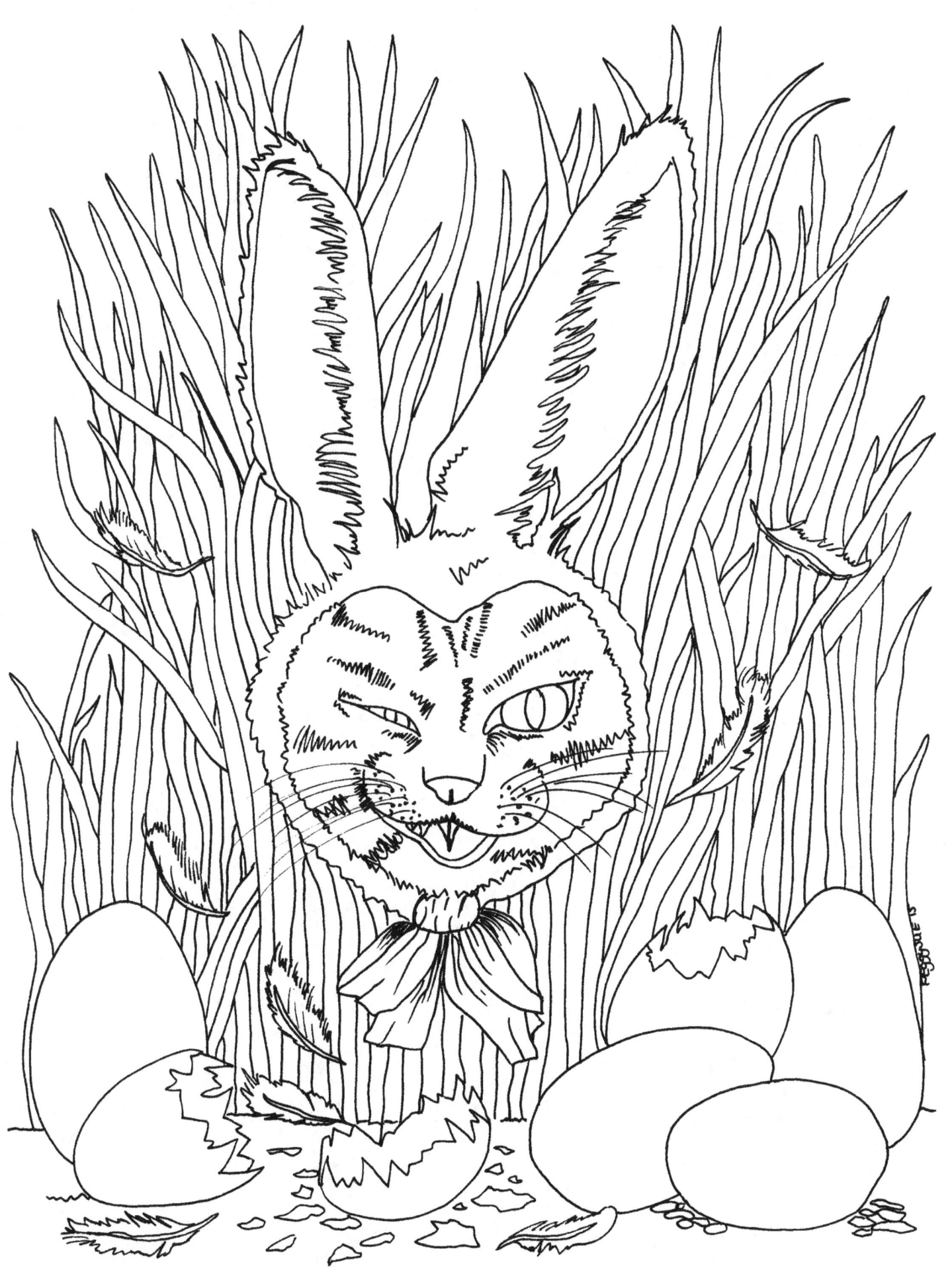

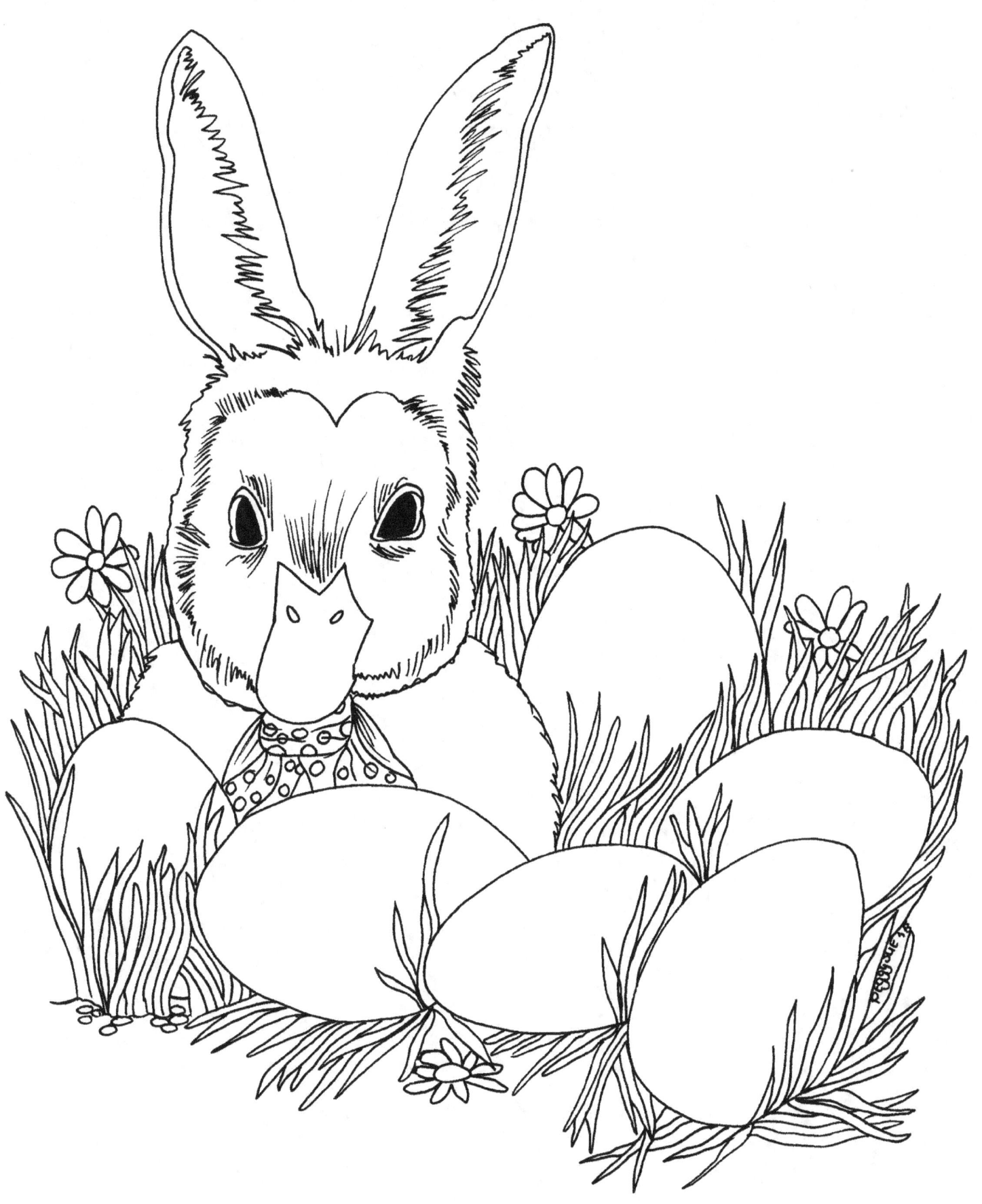

Contributing Artist
Nicole Whelan (Willow Hill Art)
WI, USA

Facebook : WillowHillArt
Etsy shop : WillowHillArt

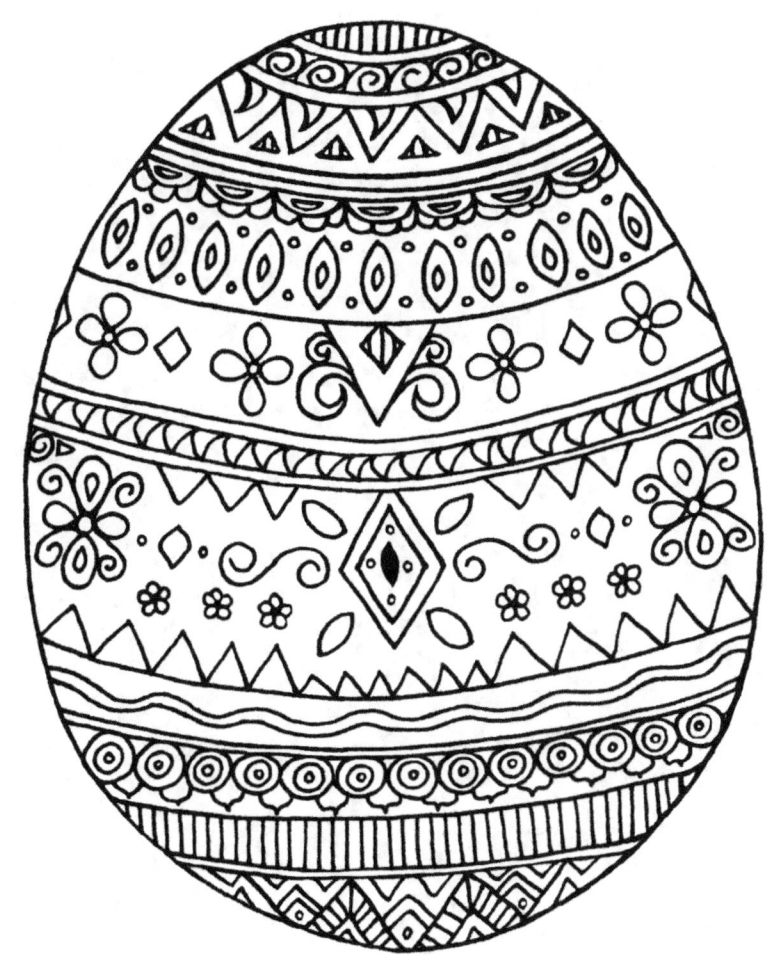
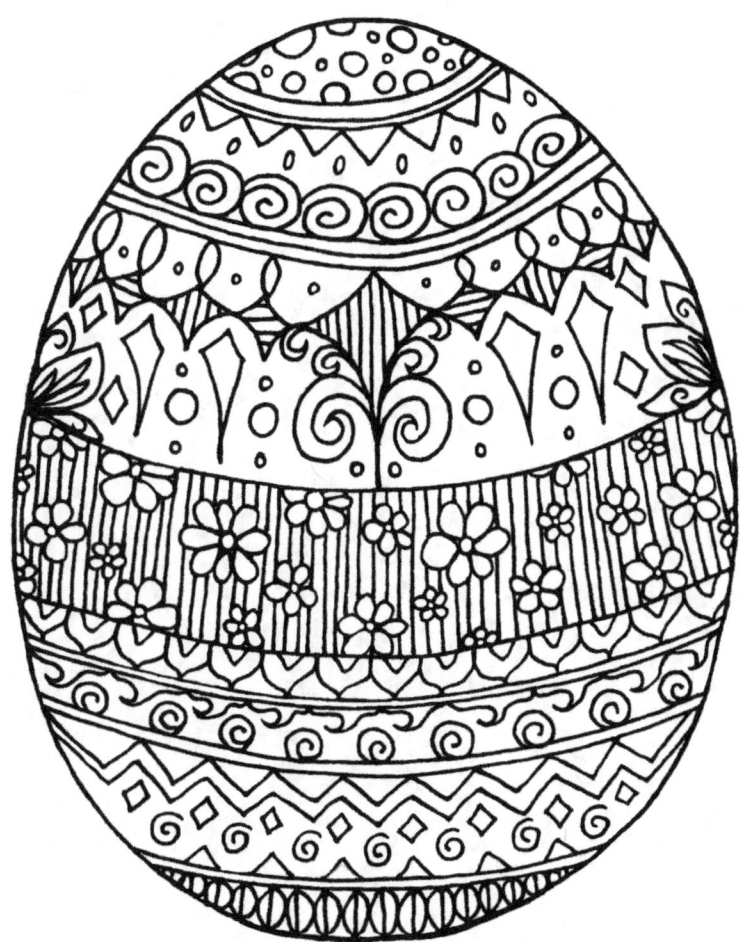

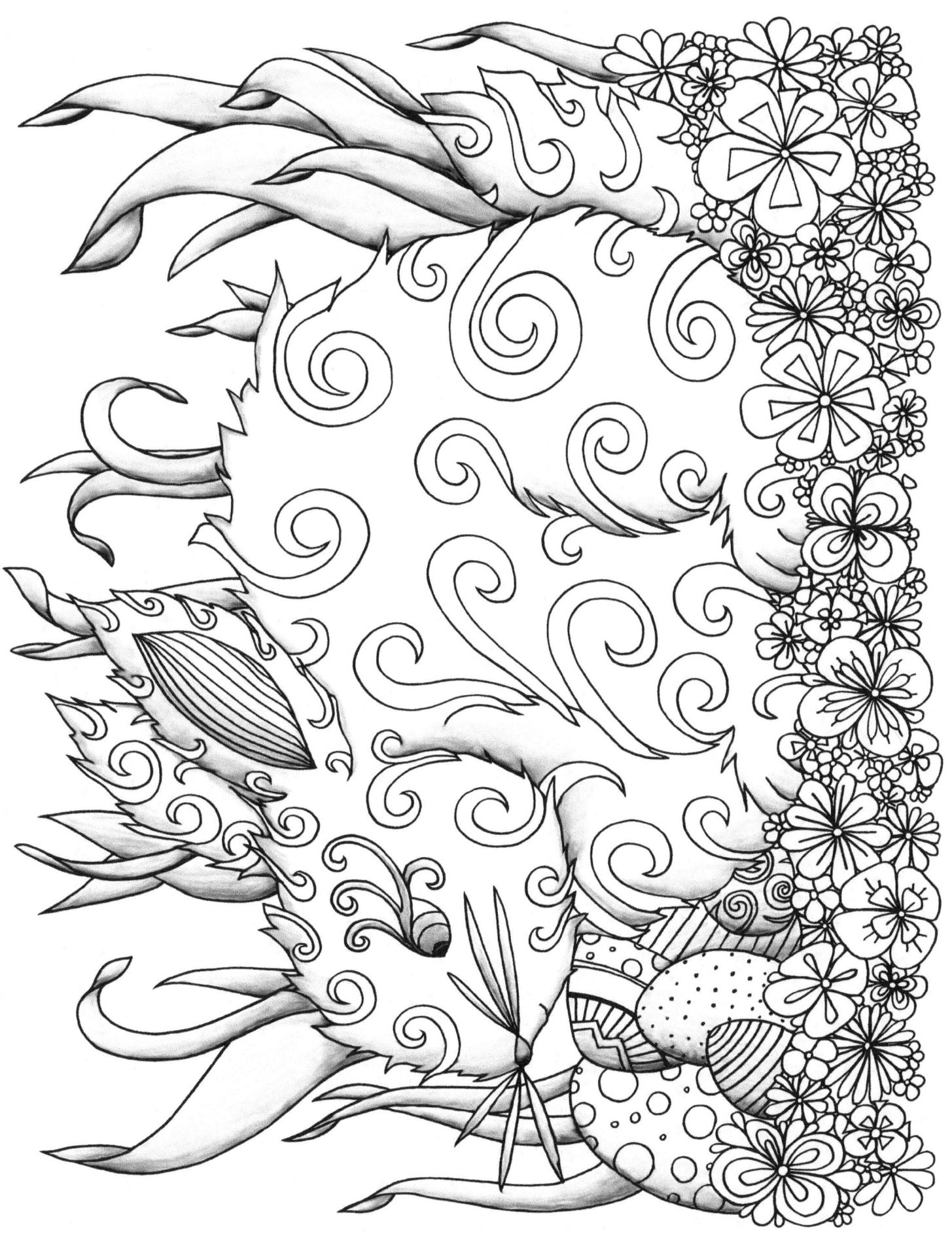

Contributing Artist
Adriana Graciela Volpe
Argentina

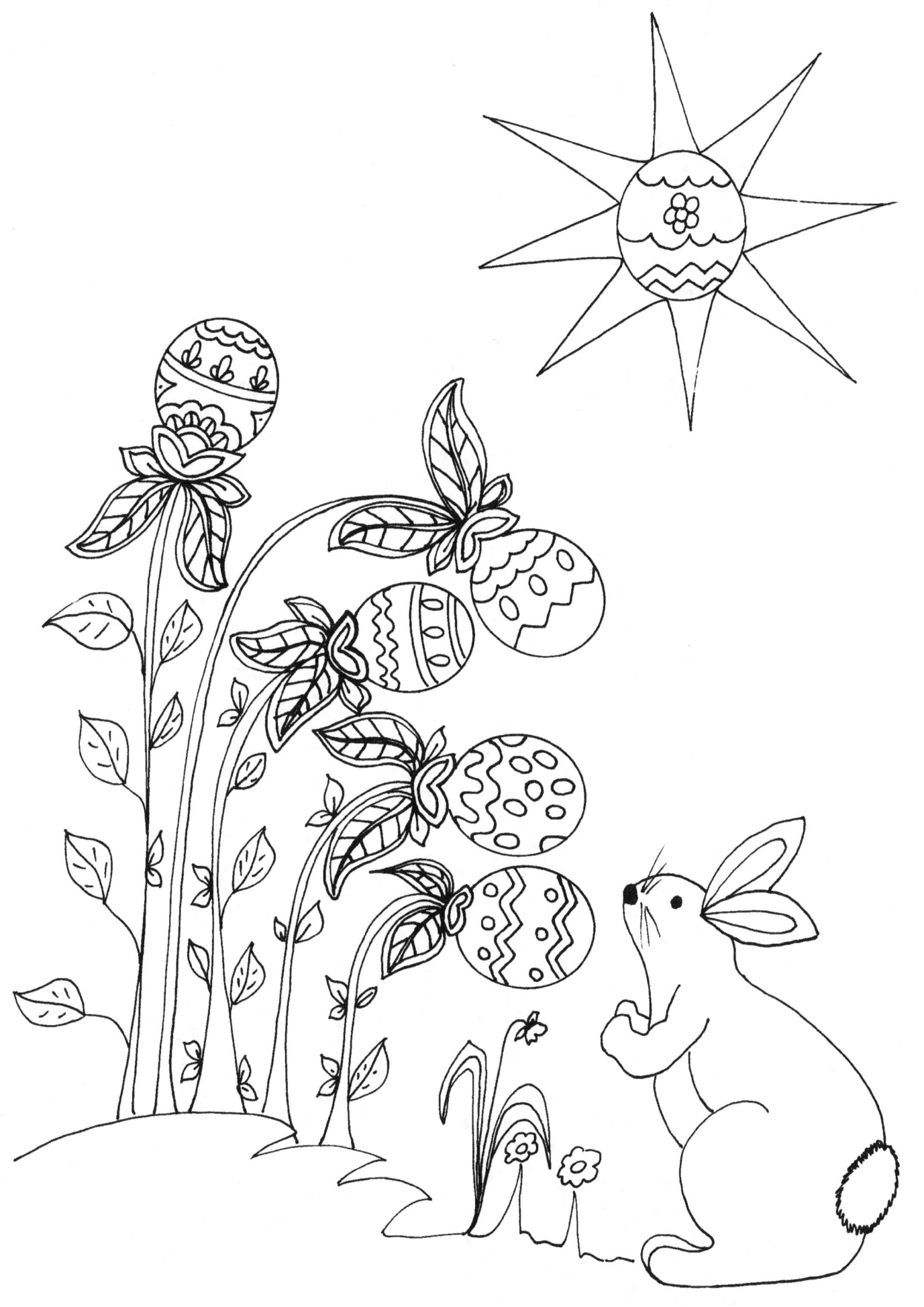

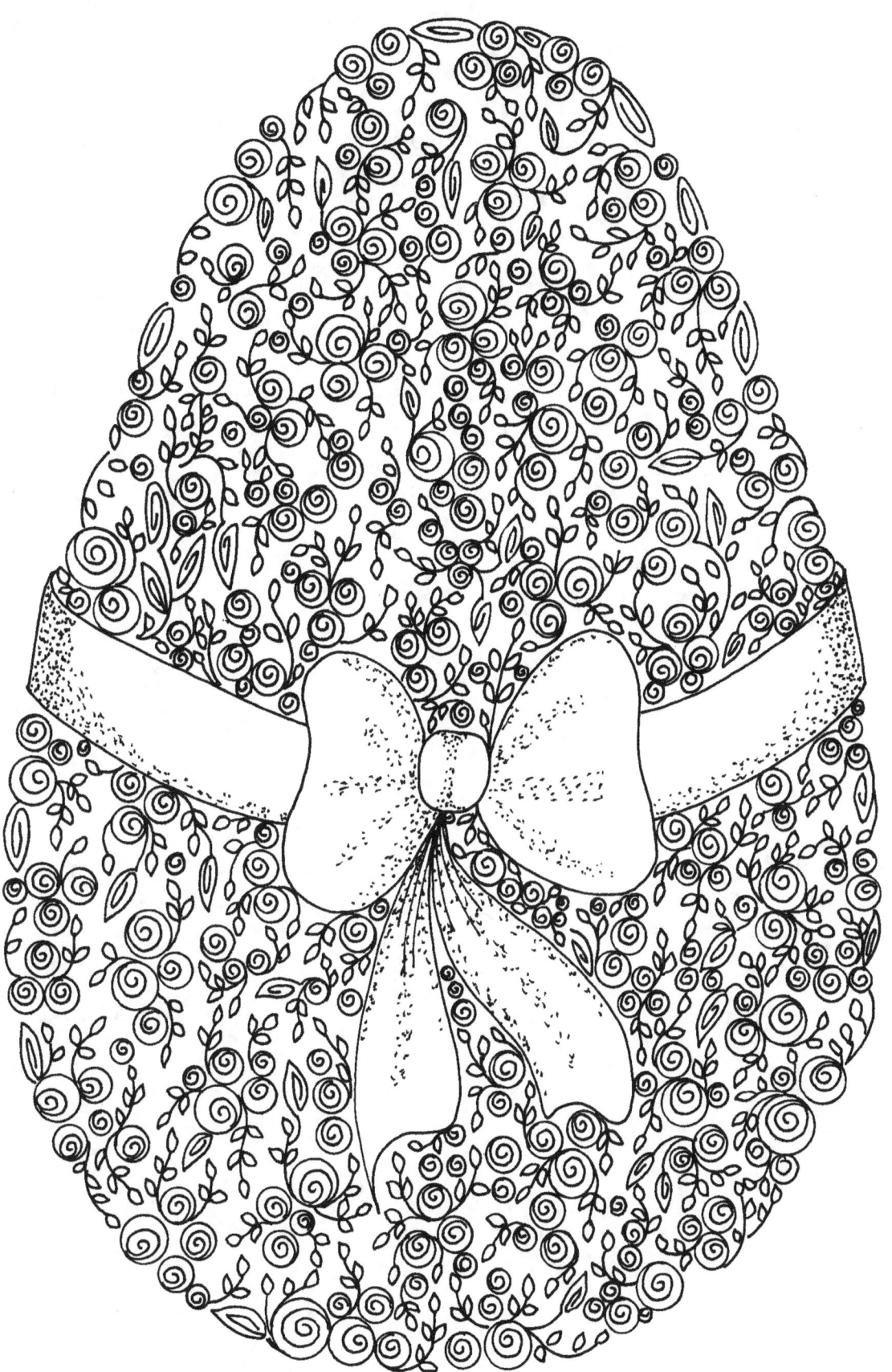

Contributing Artist
Hung Ai-Ling
Taiwan

Facebook : inspiredartLing

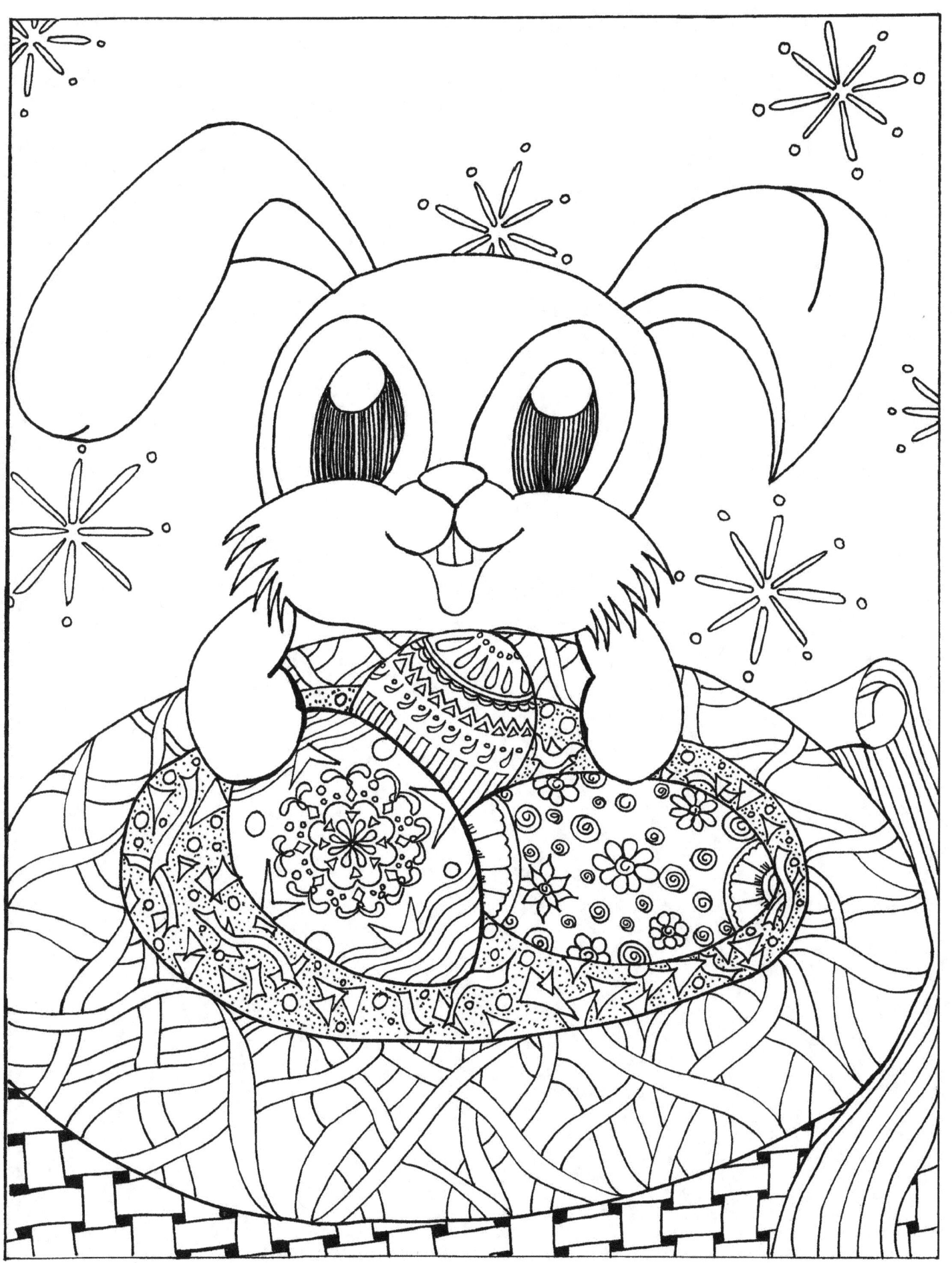

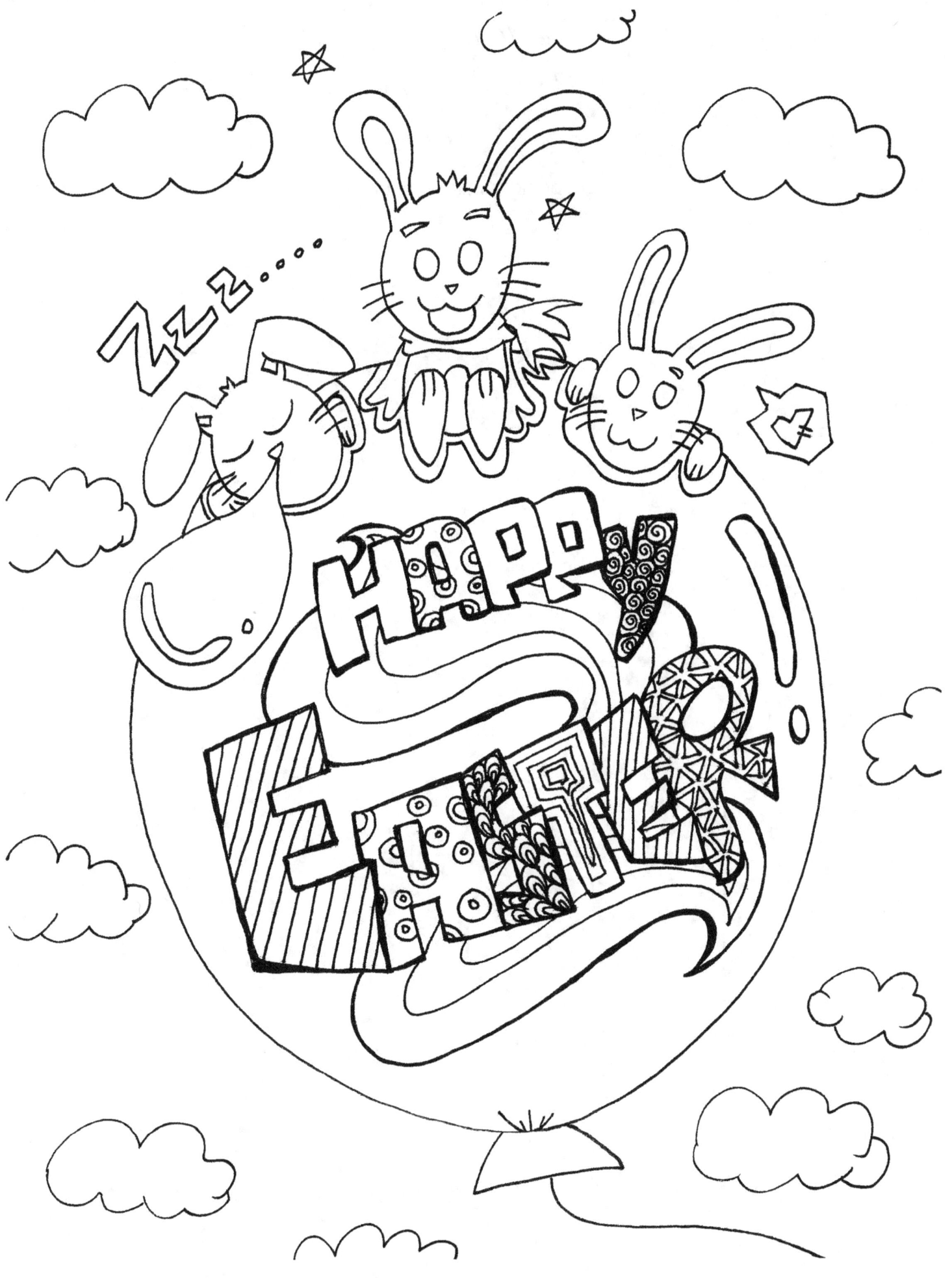

Contributing Artist
Arianne Schimmel
The Netherlands

Facebook : ArianneSchimmel

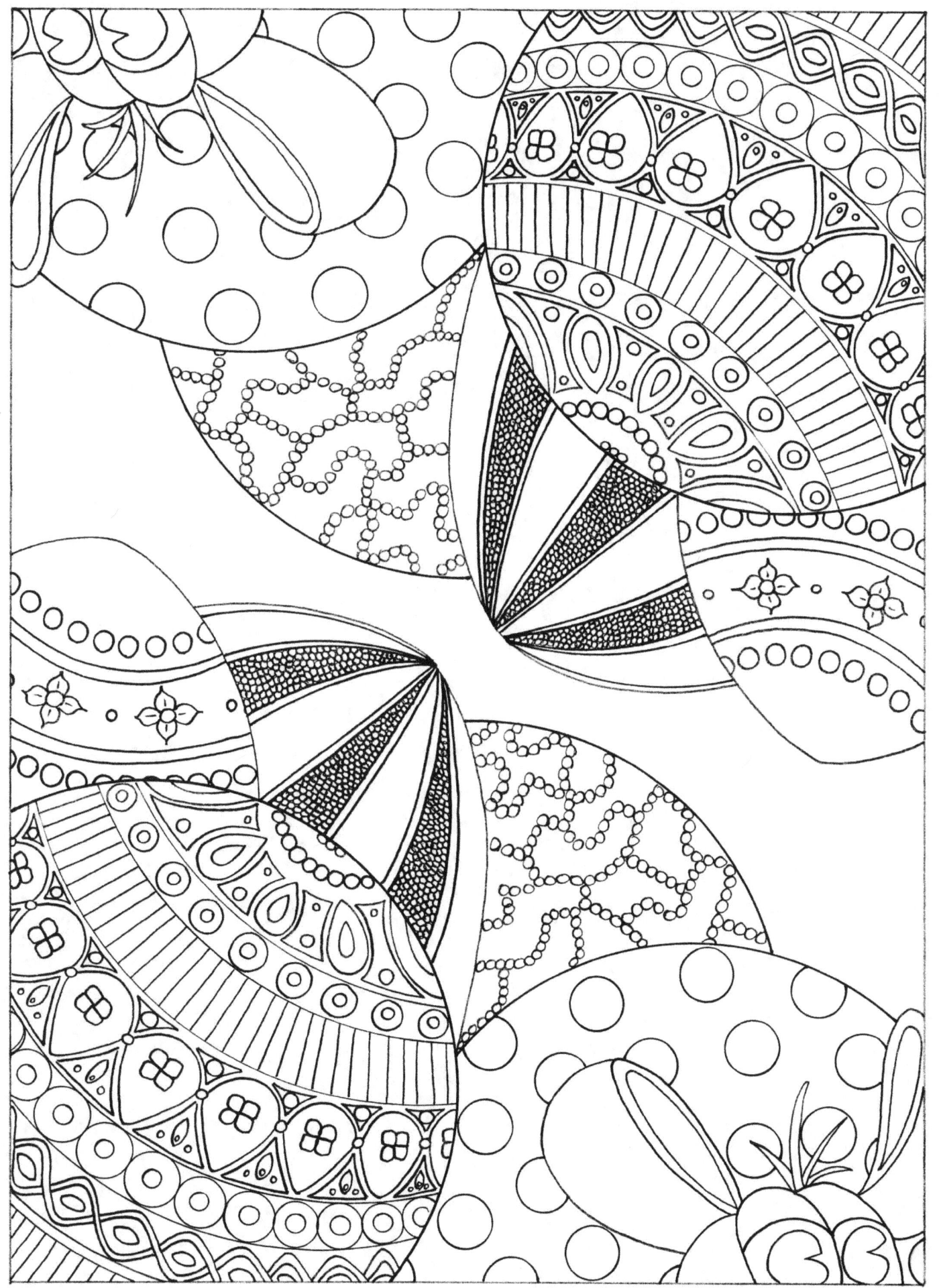

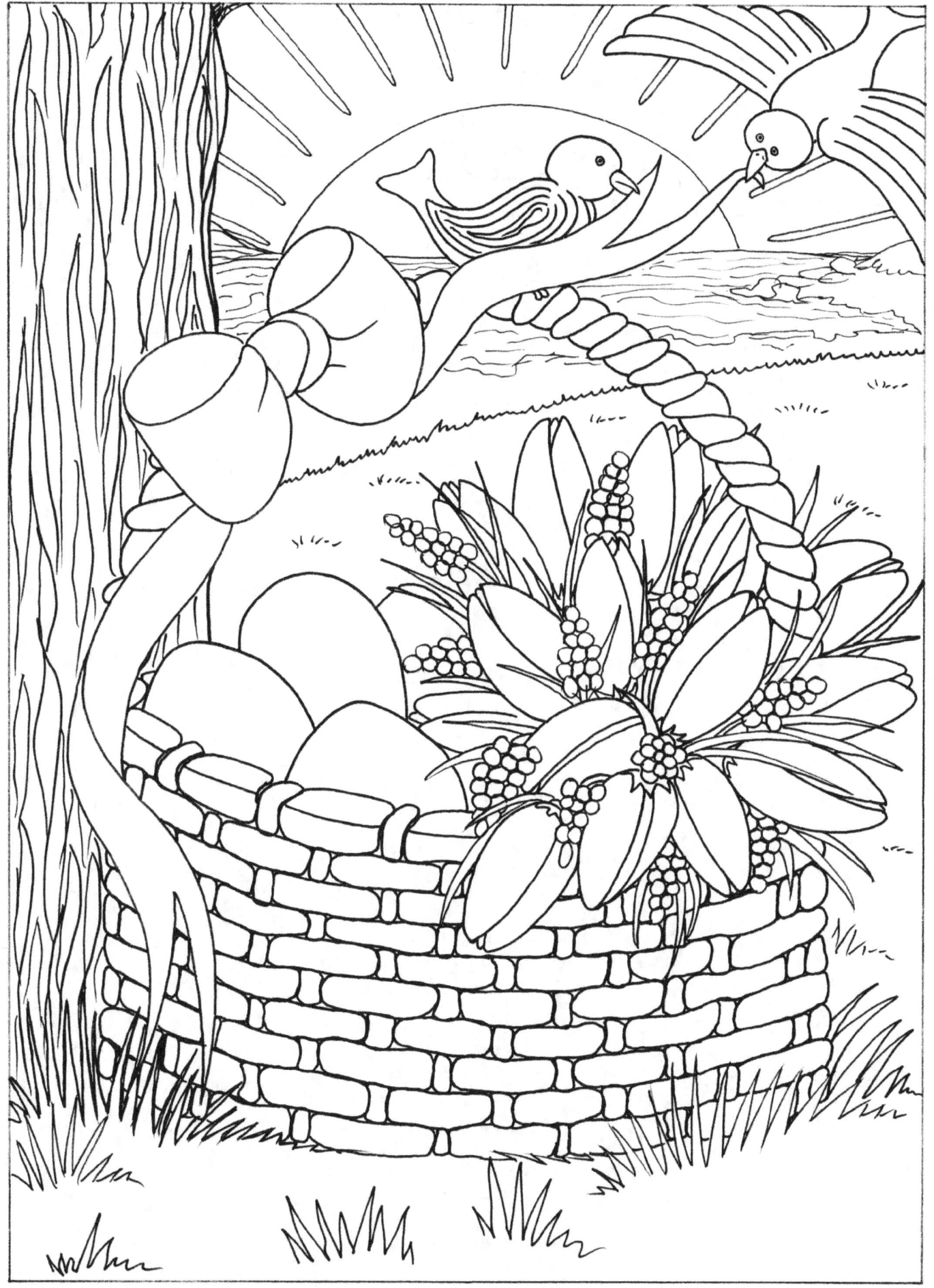

Contributing Artist
Isa Humeau
France

Facebook : graphizen

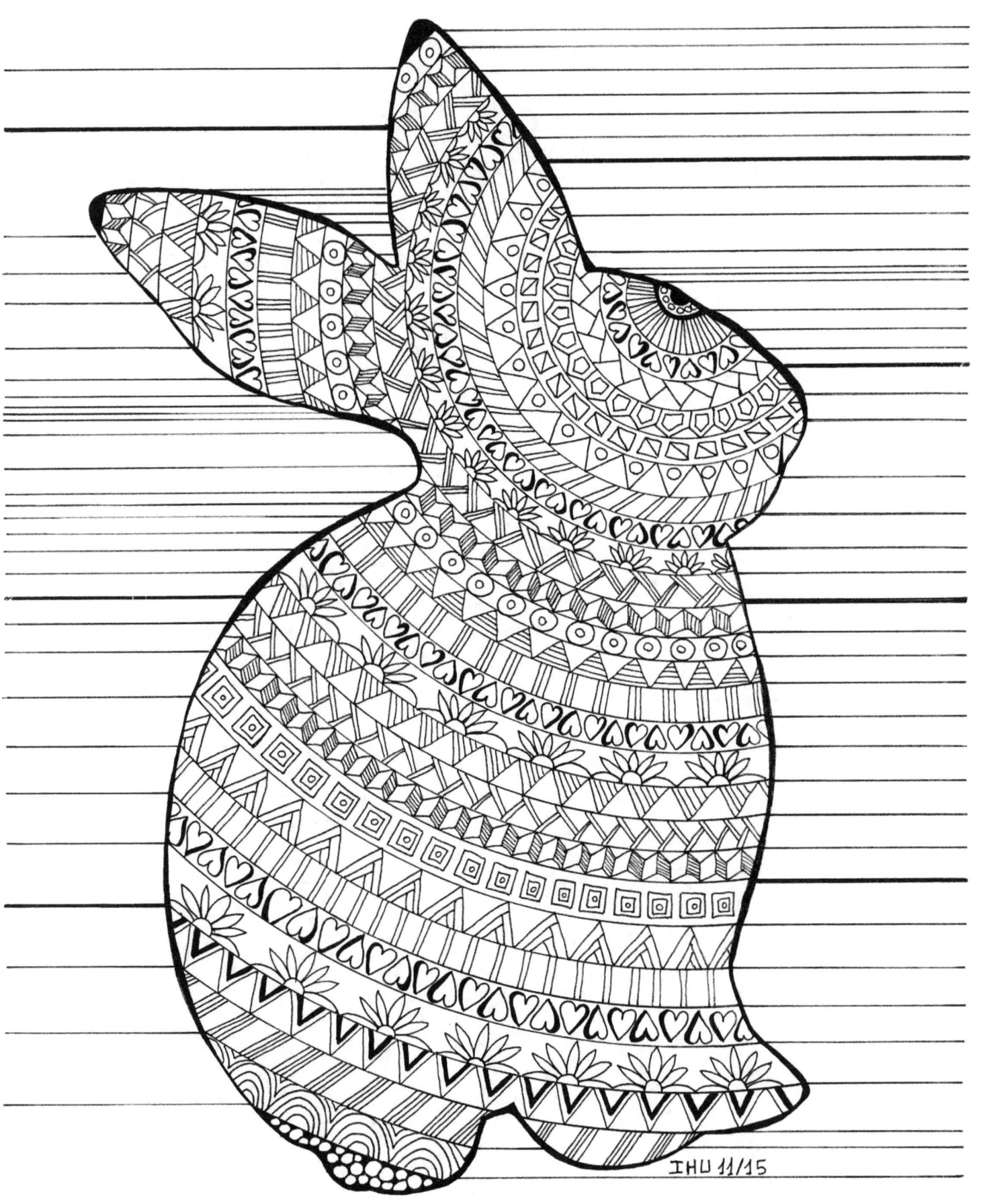

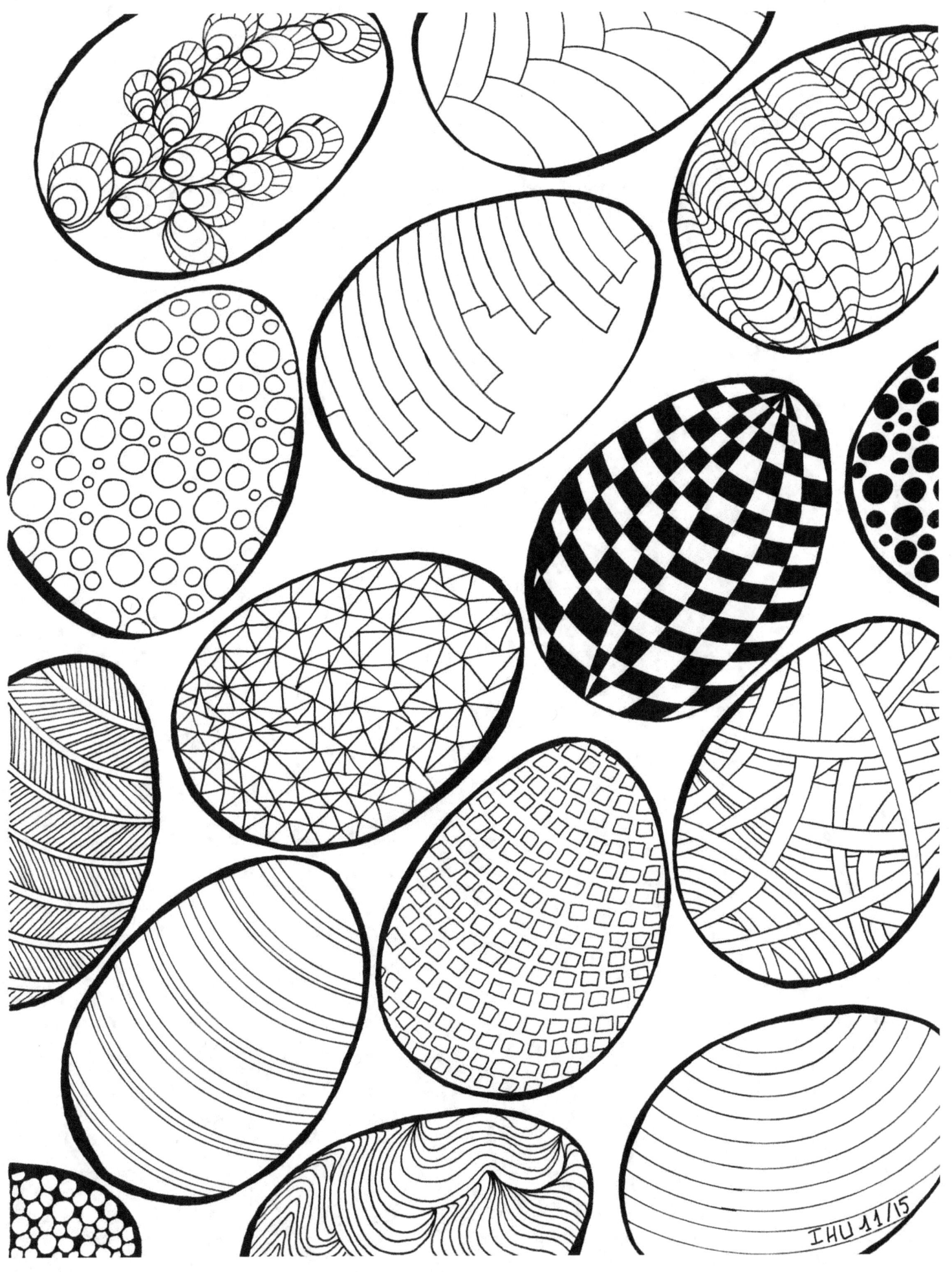

Contributing Artist
Heather Richards
USA

http://www.teacherspayteachers.com/store/TruthMe

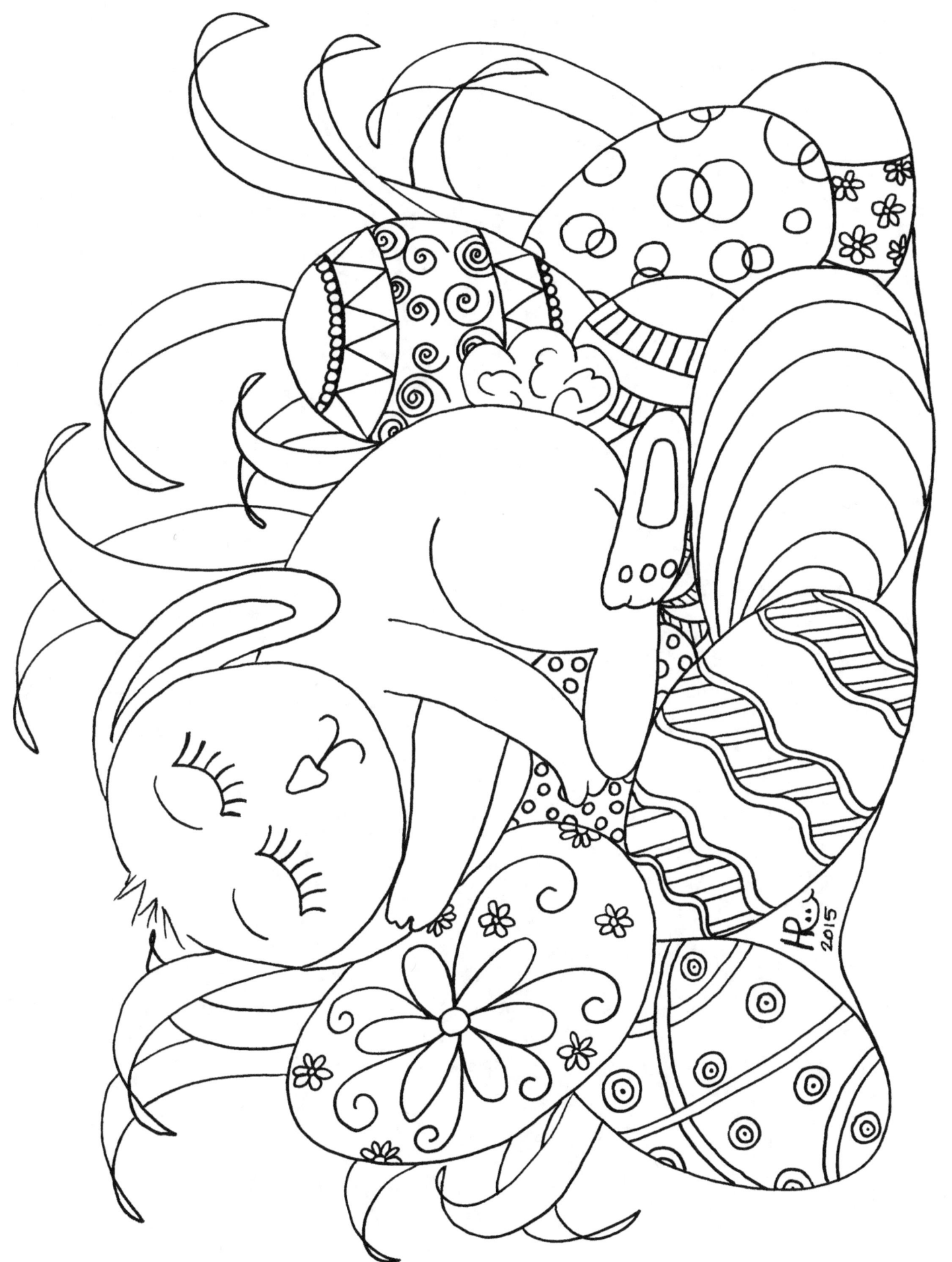

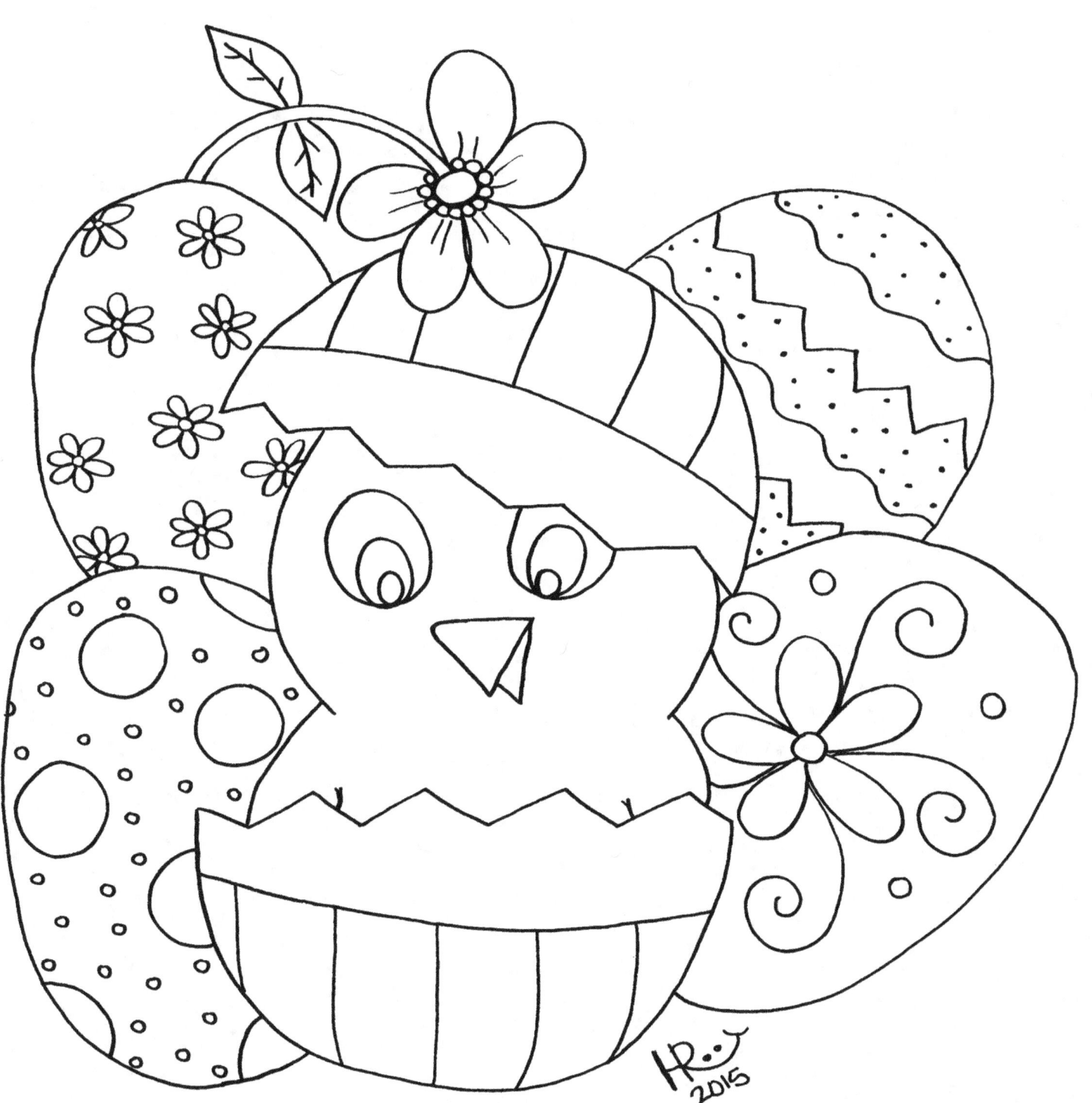

Contributing Artist
Sabine Design
The Netherlands

Facebook : Sabine-Design

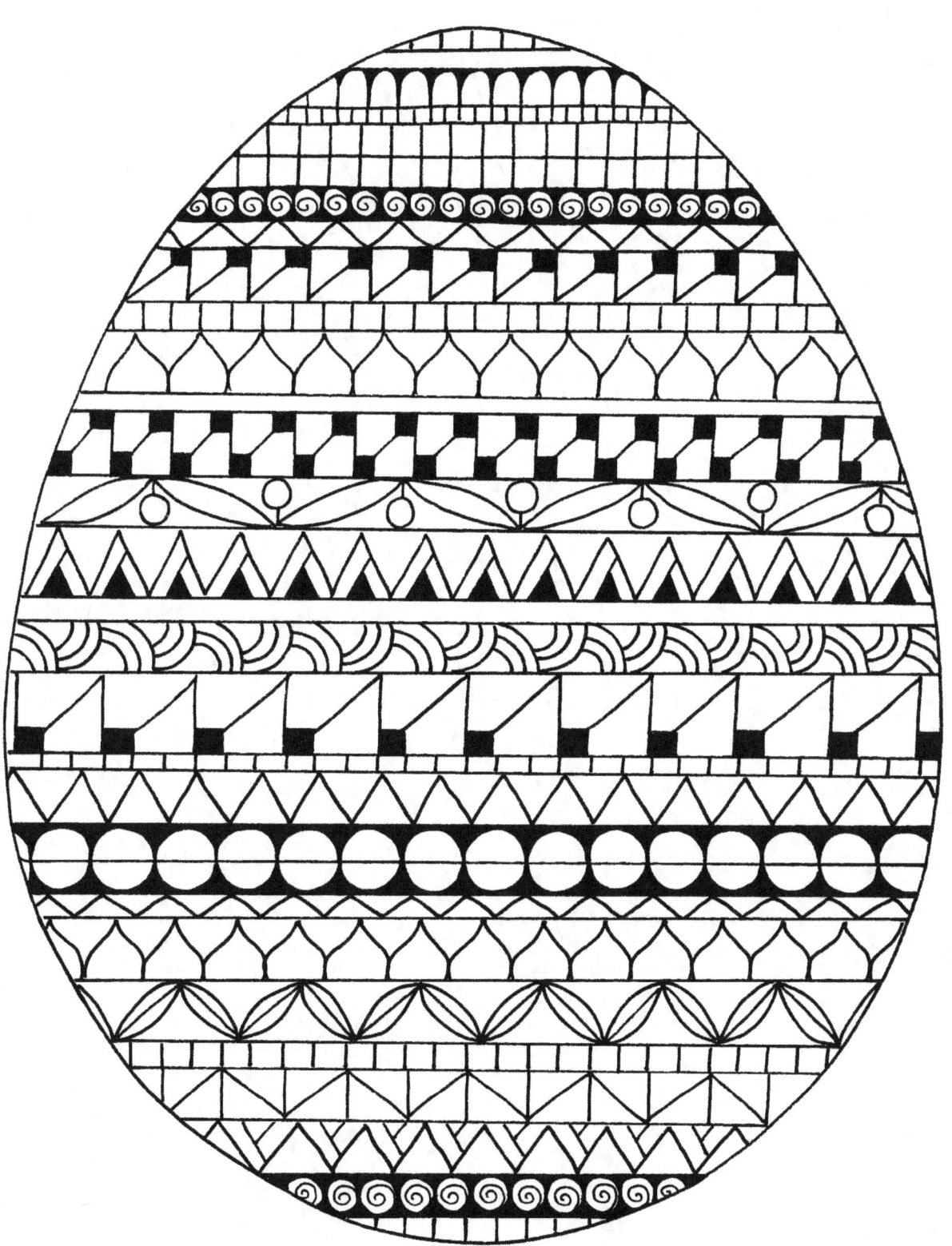

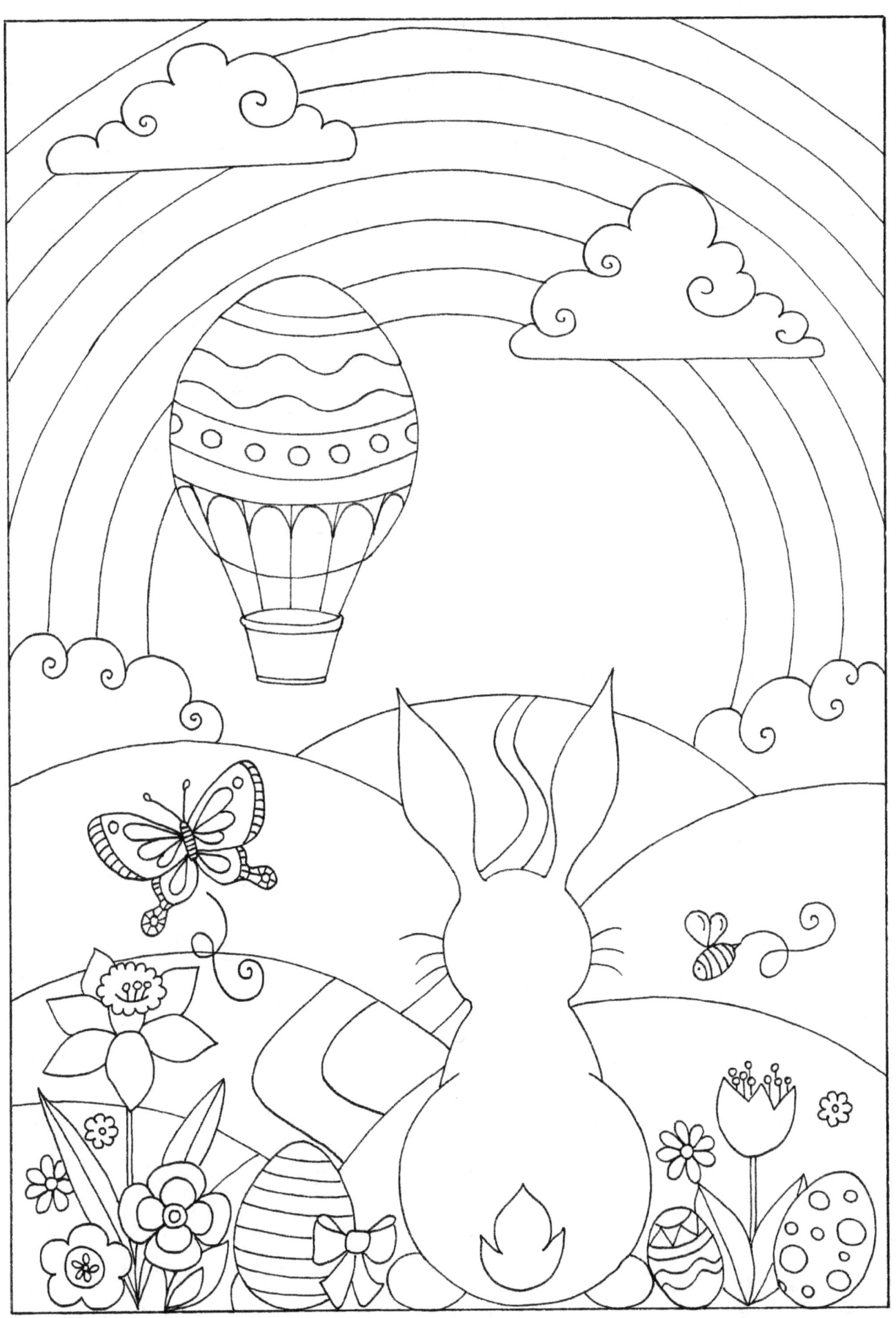

Contributing Artist
Laurie Beauchamp
USA

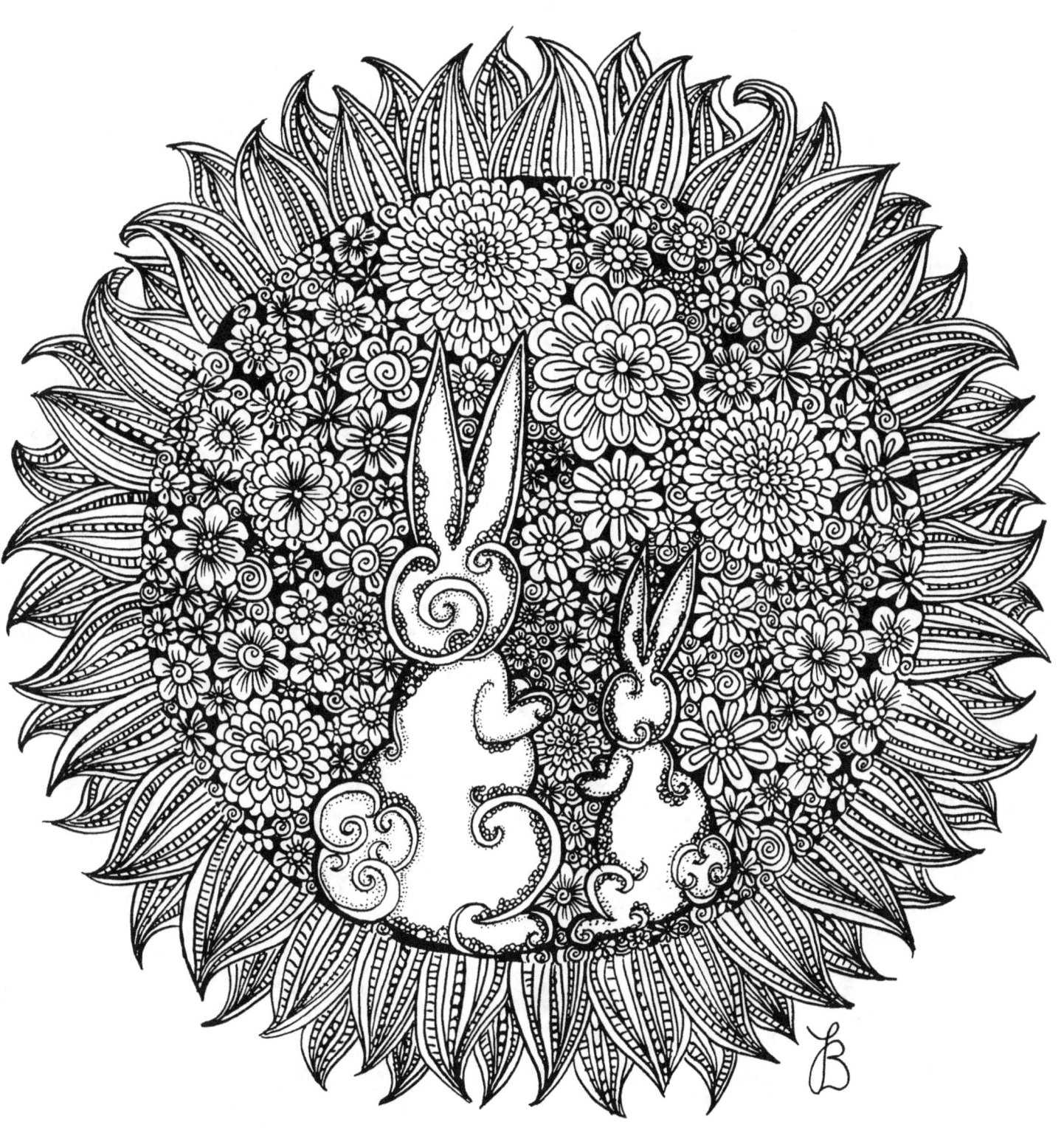

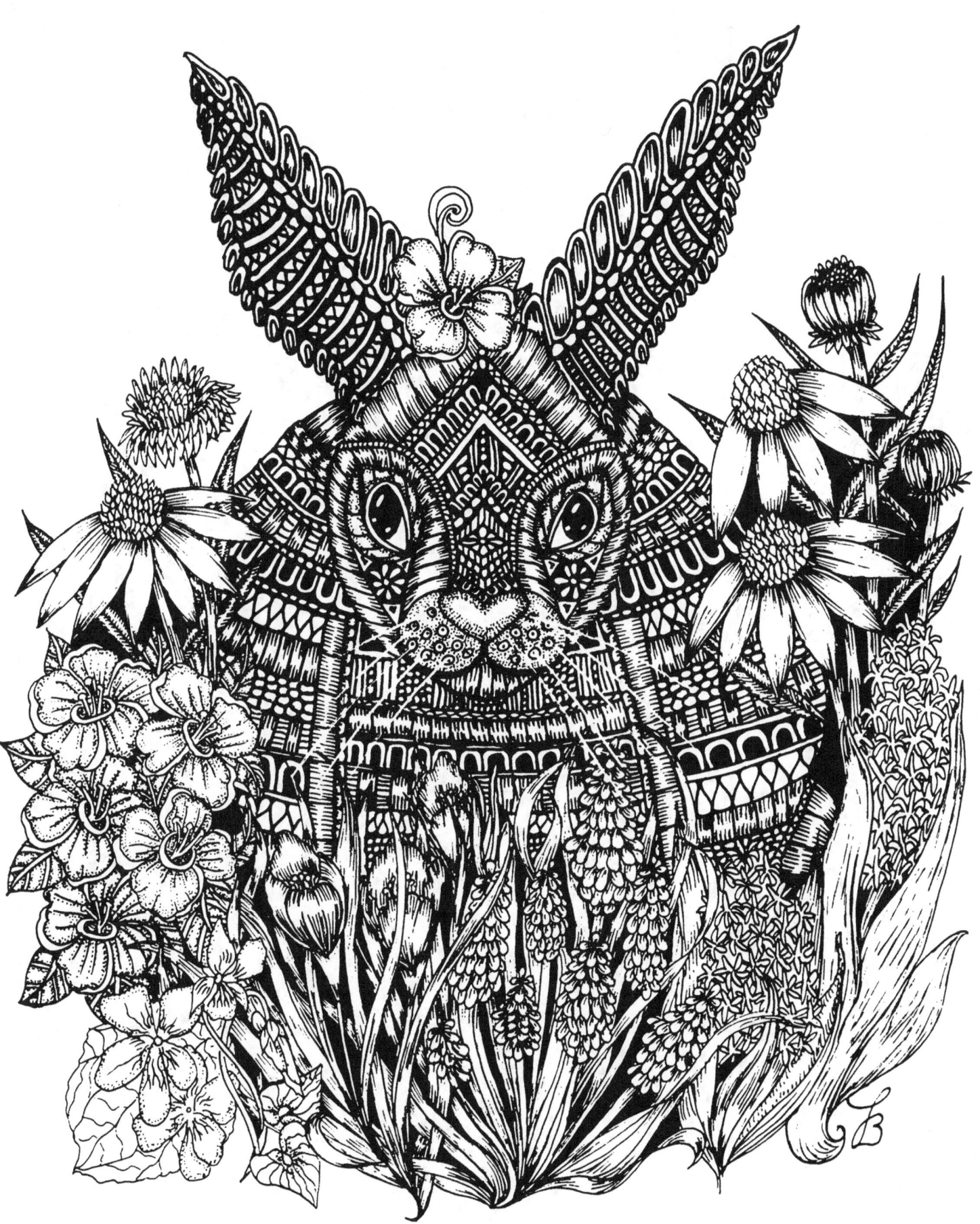

Contributing Artist
Jovian Ke
Taiwan

Facebook : JK.Illustration

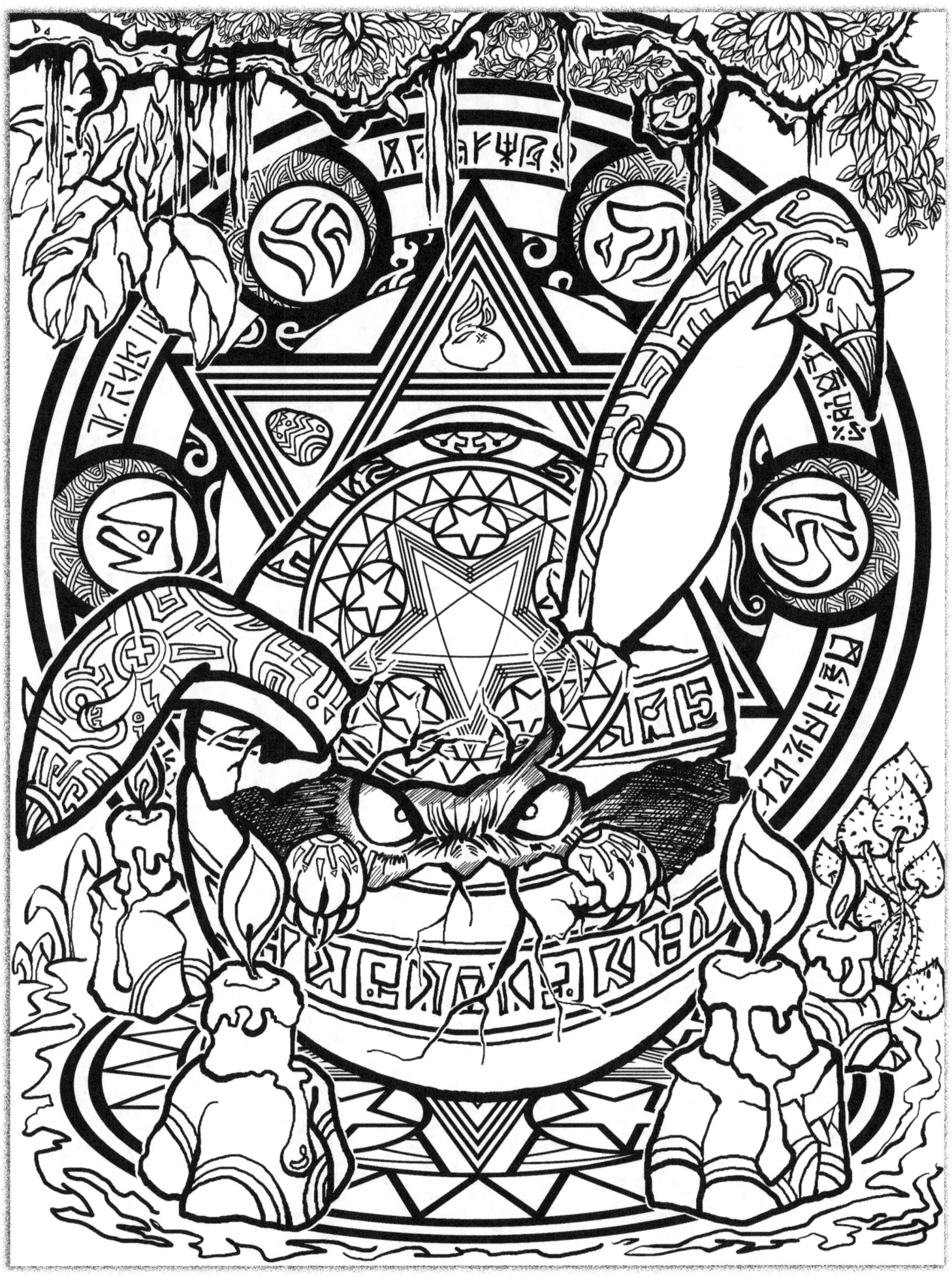

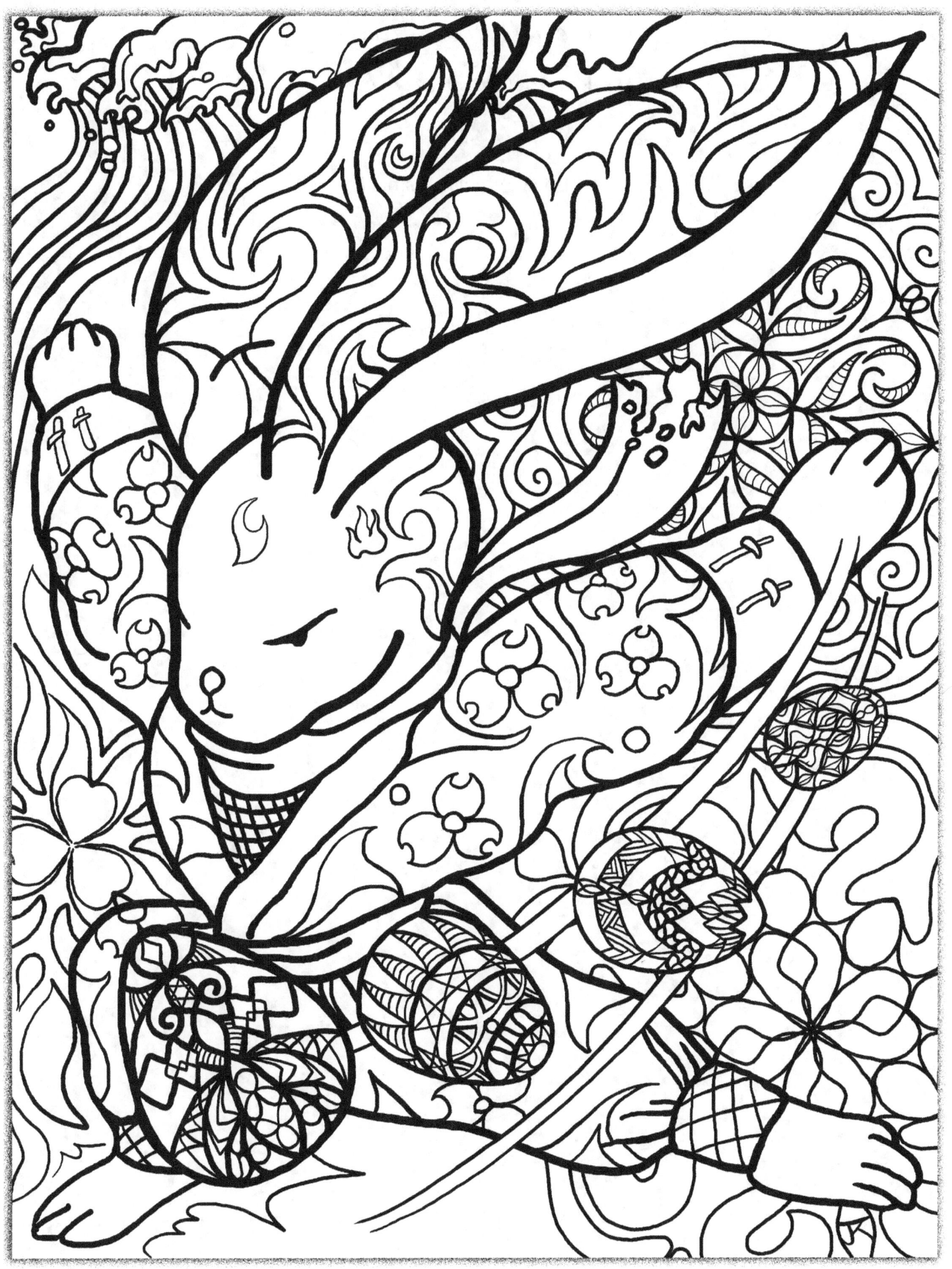

Contributing Artist
Wenyu Lin Small Fish
Taiwan

Facebook : smallfish.smallfish

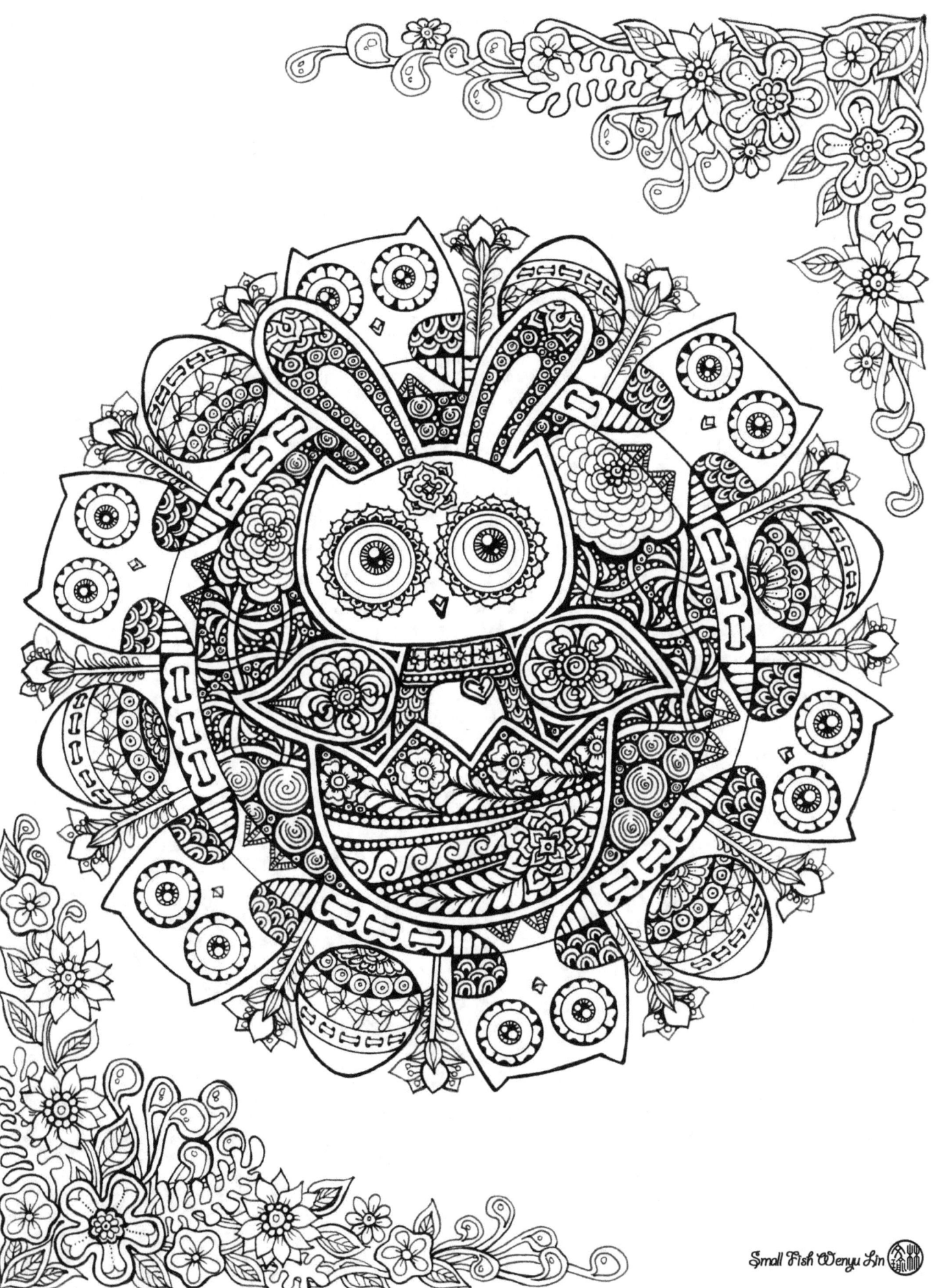

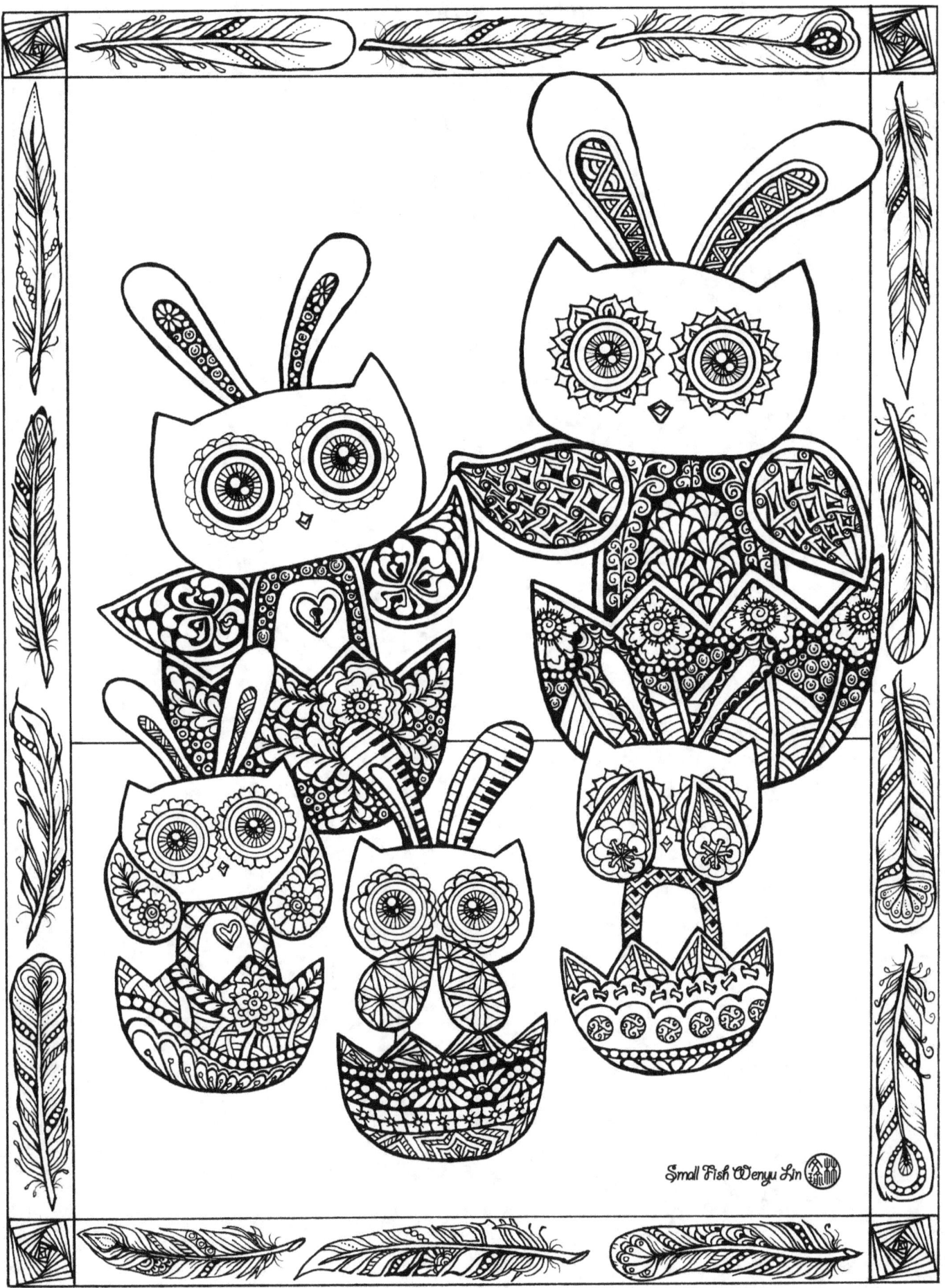

Contributing Artist
Angel Huang
Taiwan

Facebook : An99.Art

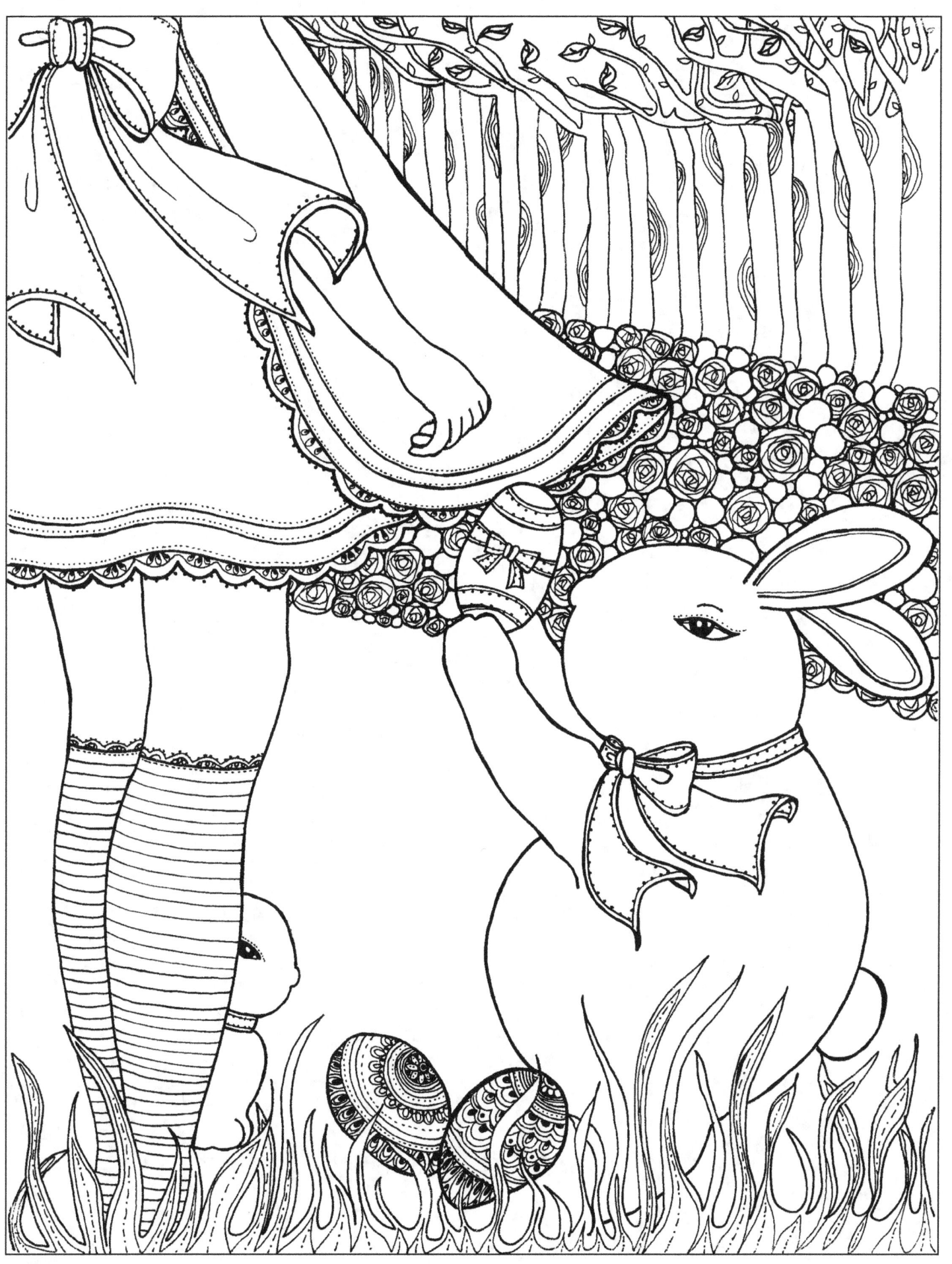

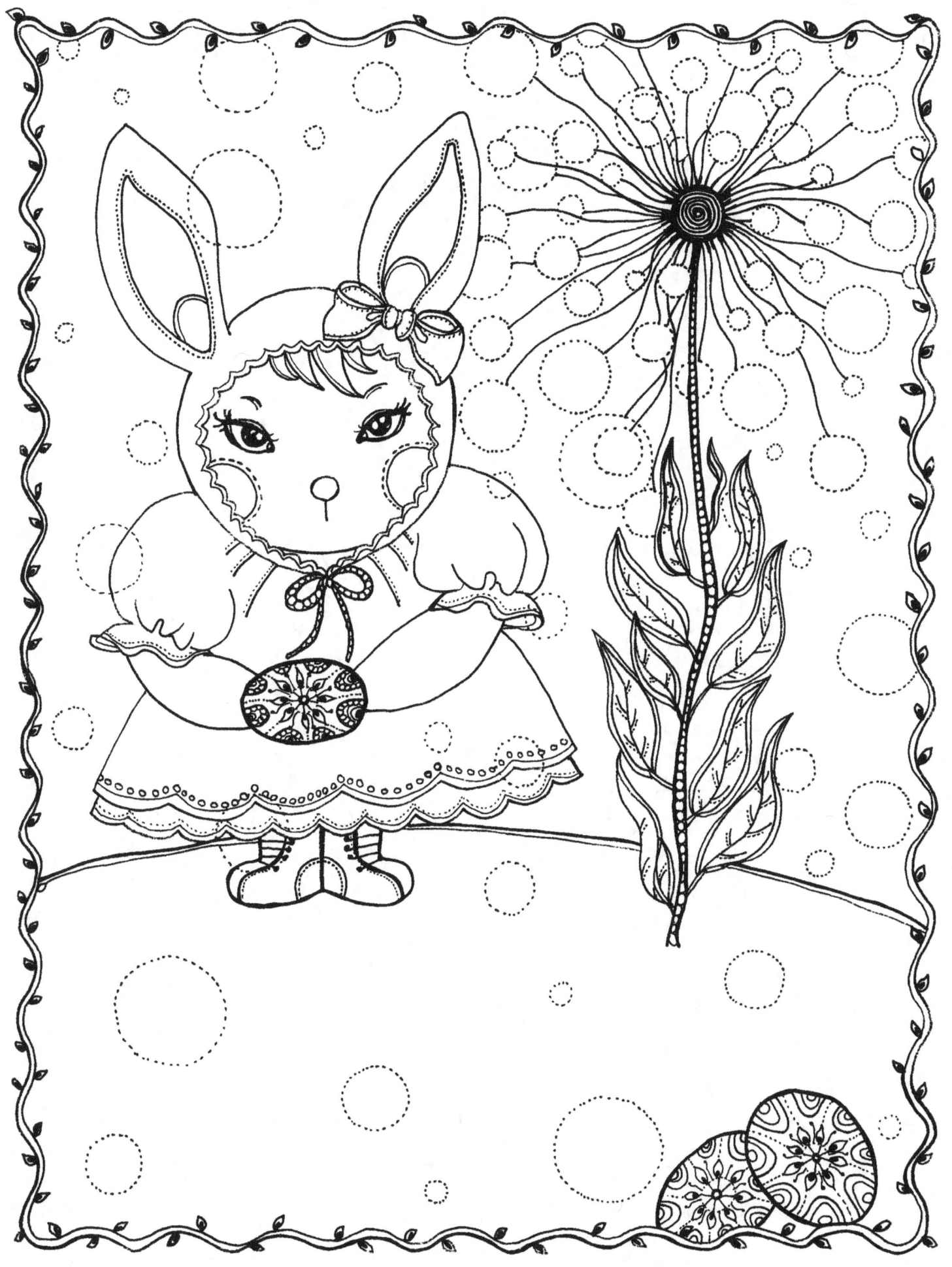

Contributing Artist
Les galaxies de 'Qi
France

Les galaxies de 'Qi

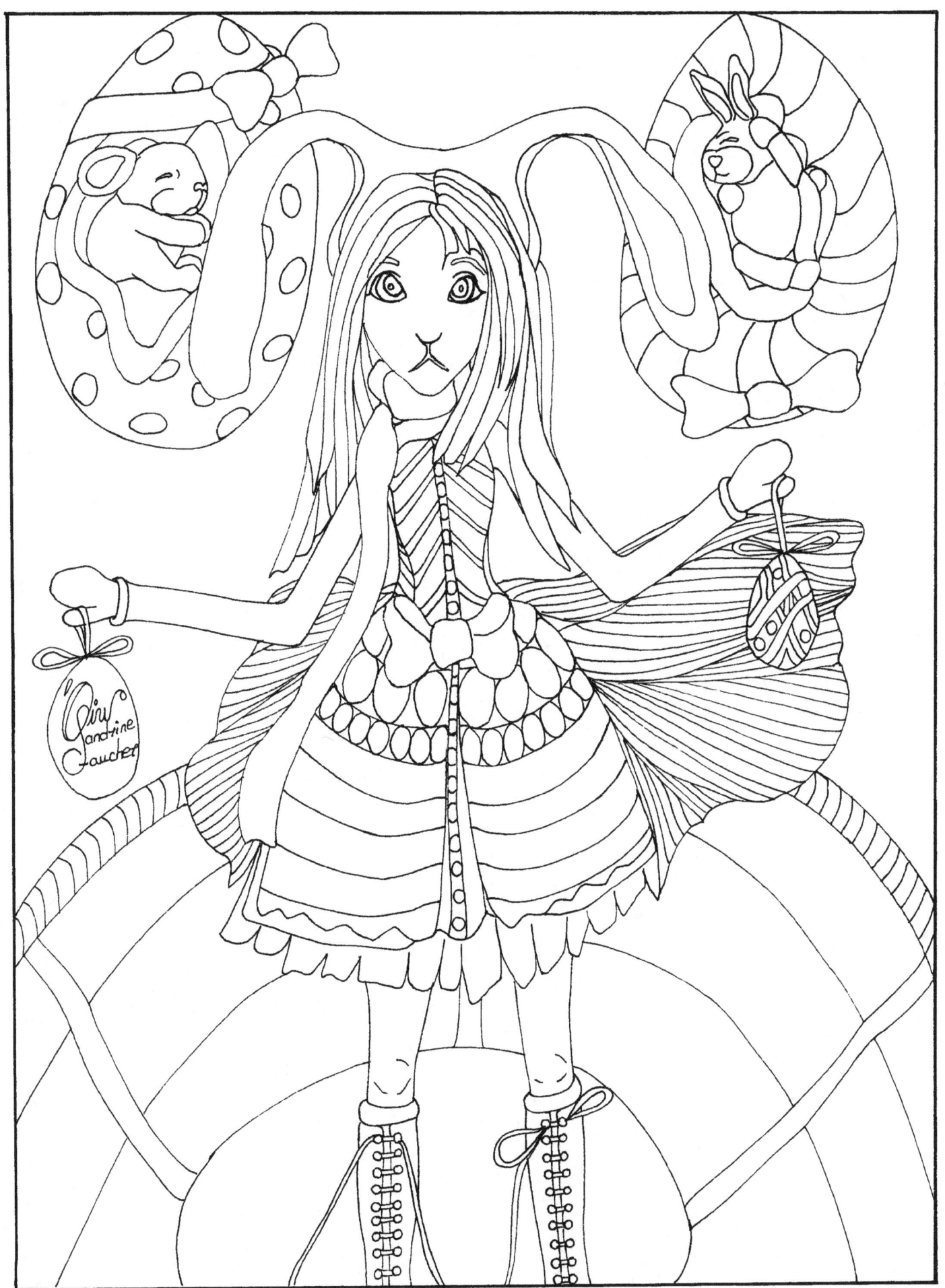

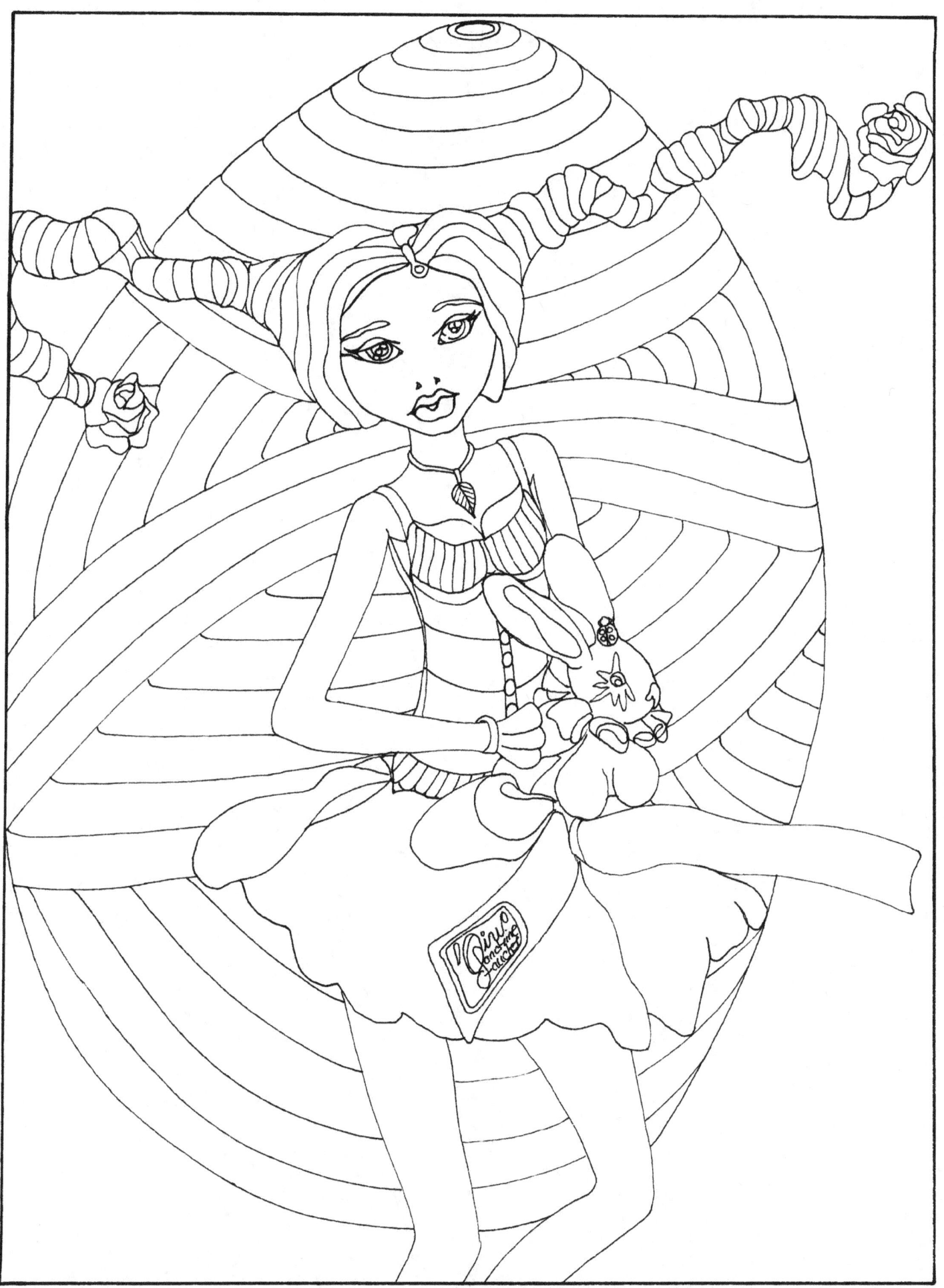

Contributing Artist
Linda Fauconnier Tricoire
France

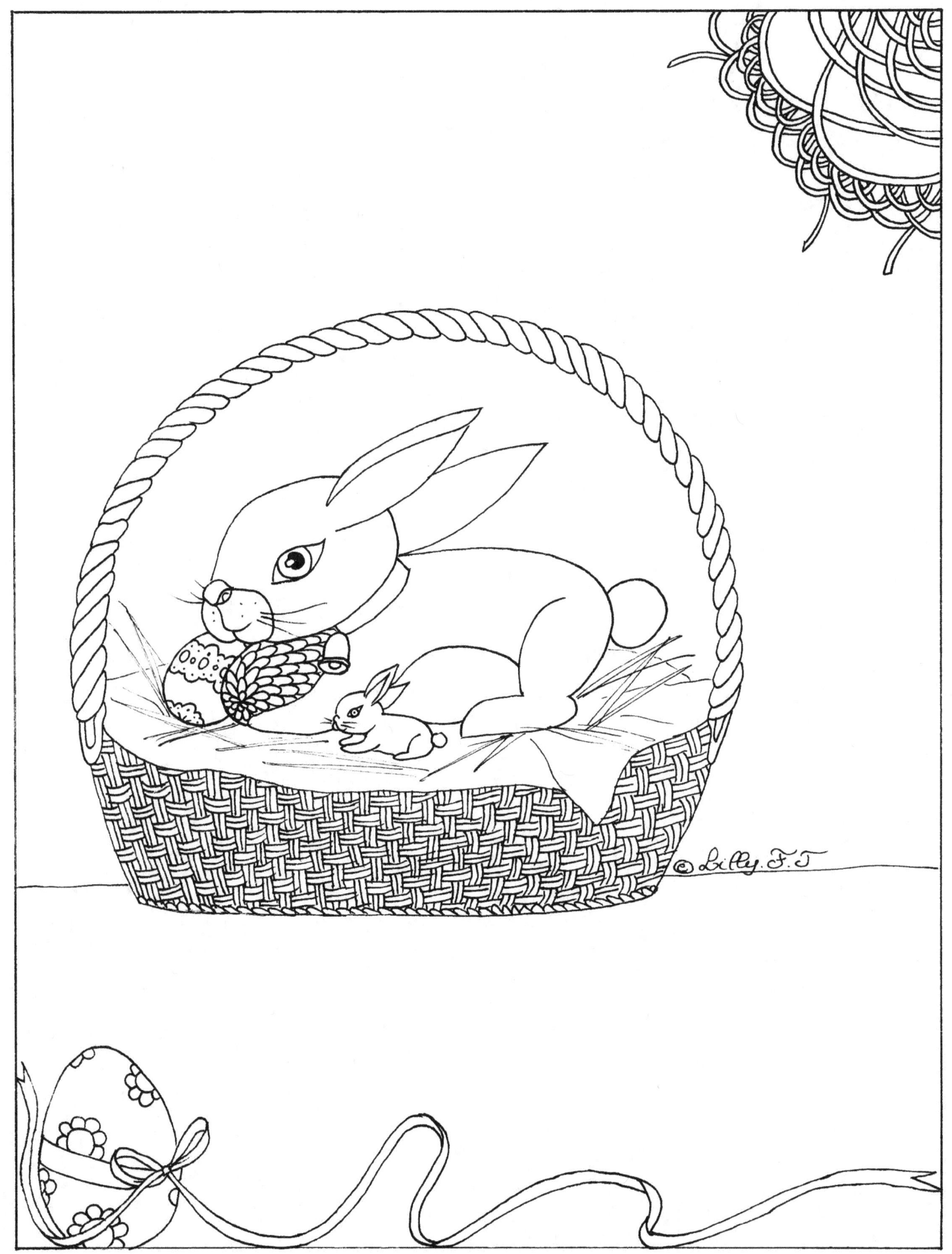

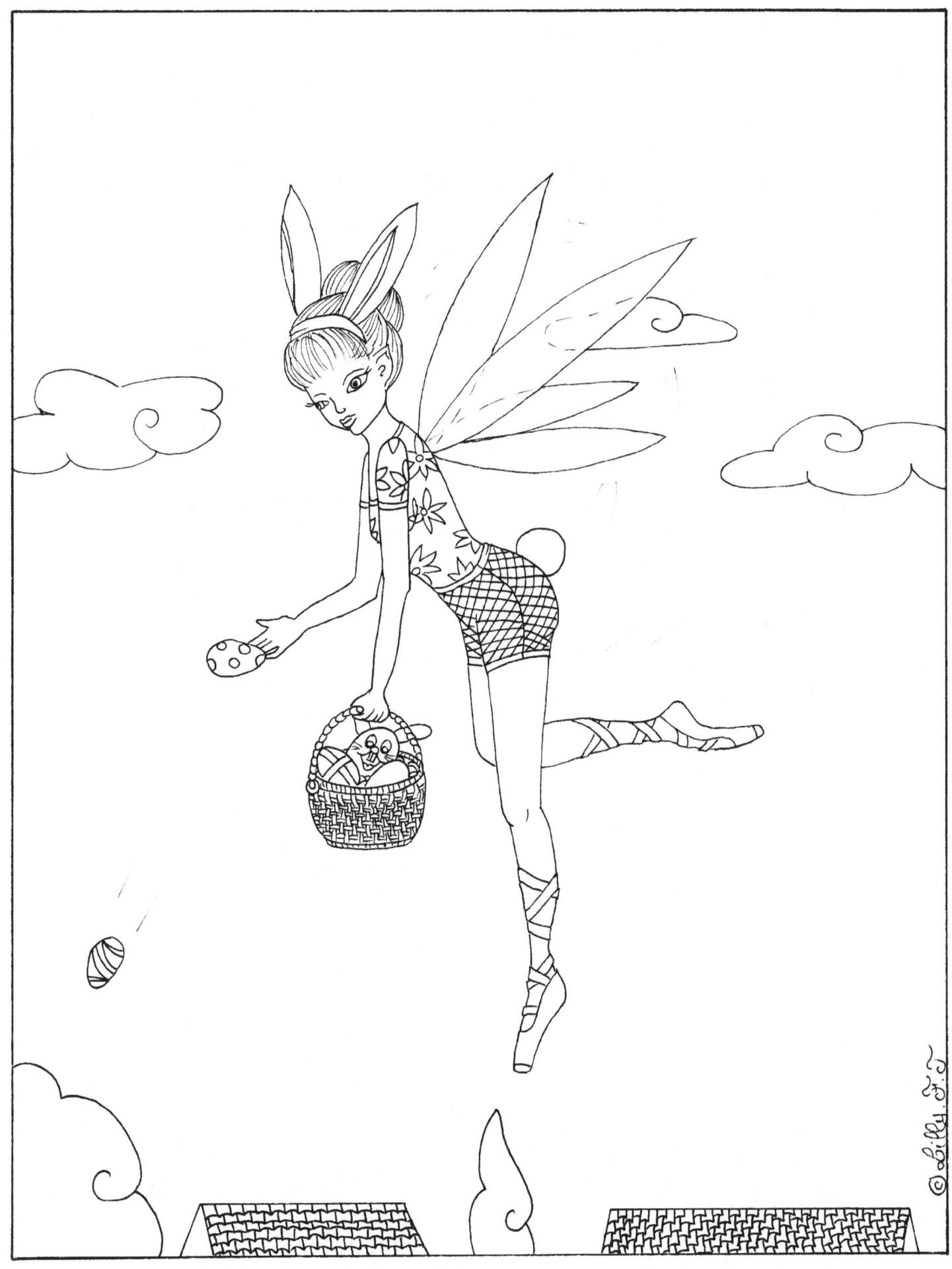

Contributing Artist
Wen Kung
Taiwan

https://www.facebook.com/Wen.Zentangle

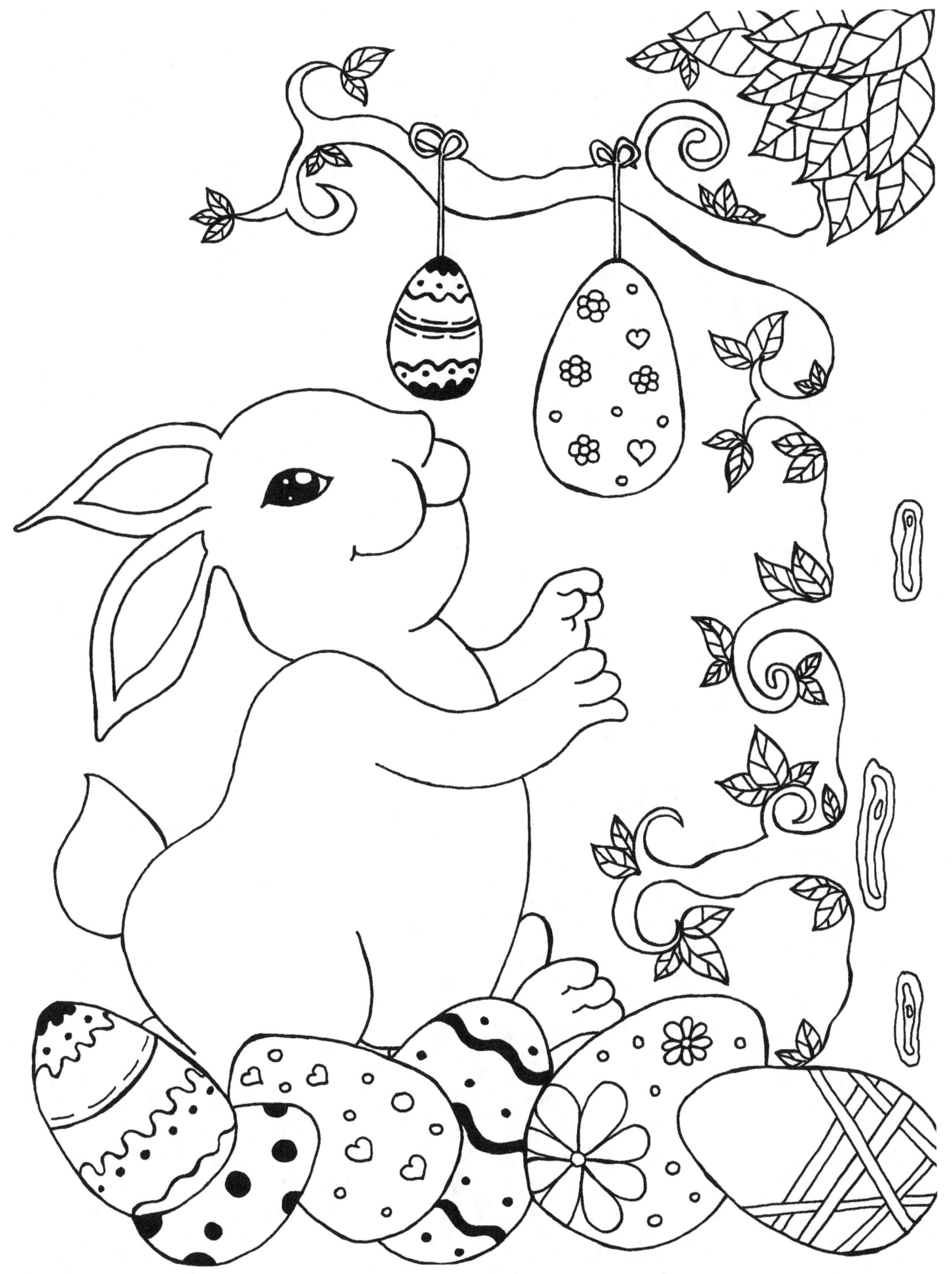

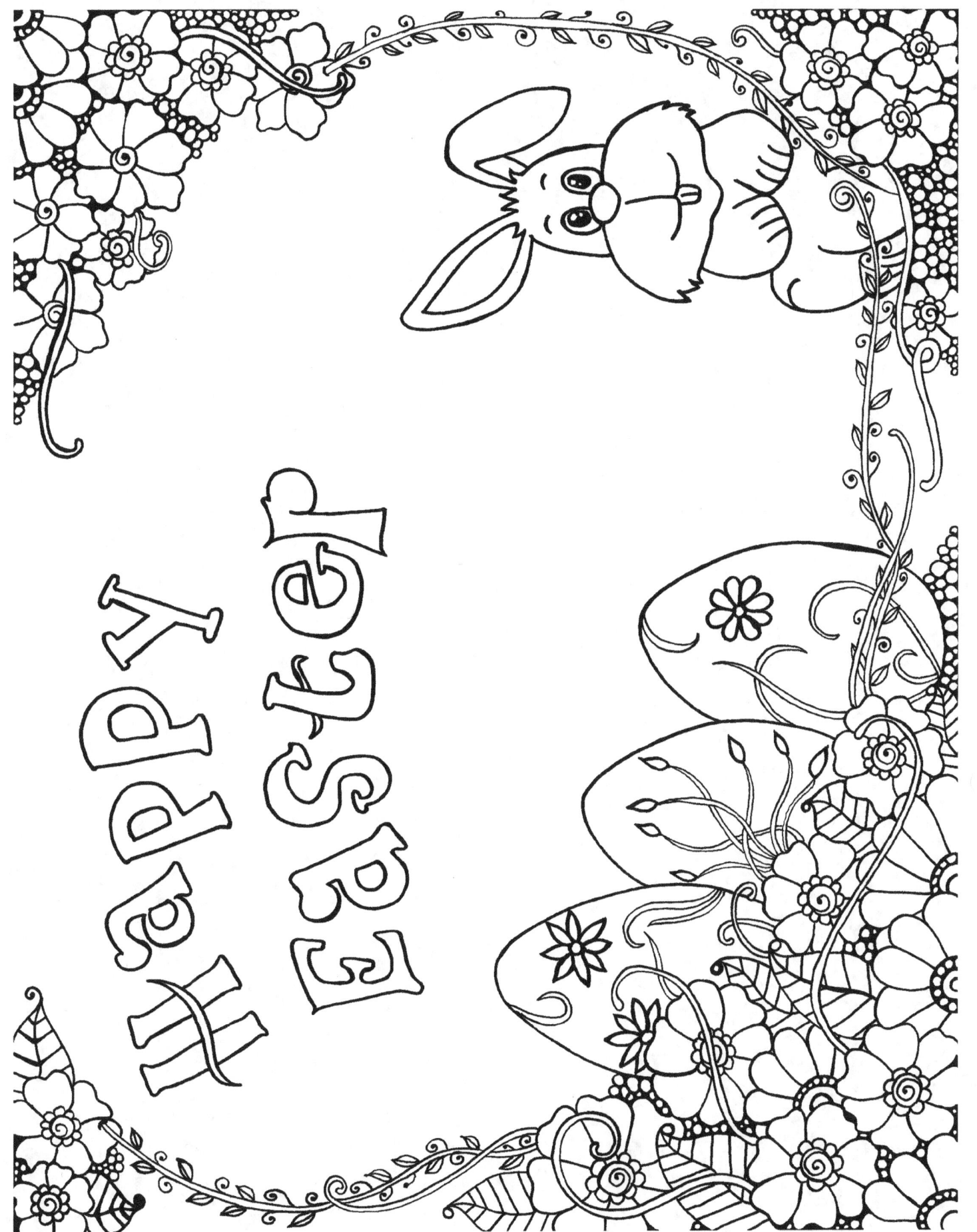

Contributing Artist
Gemeta Ling
Germany

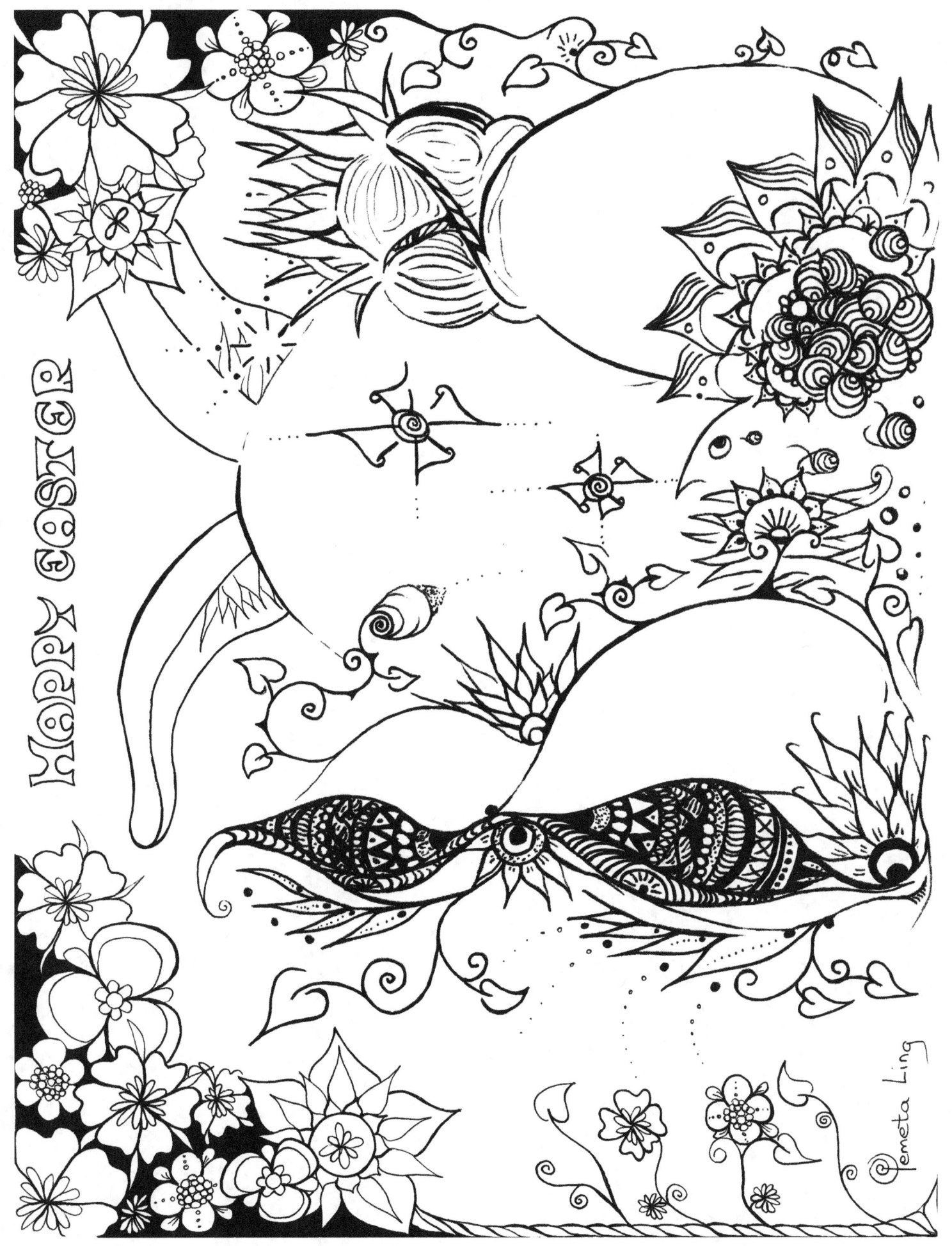

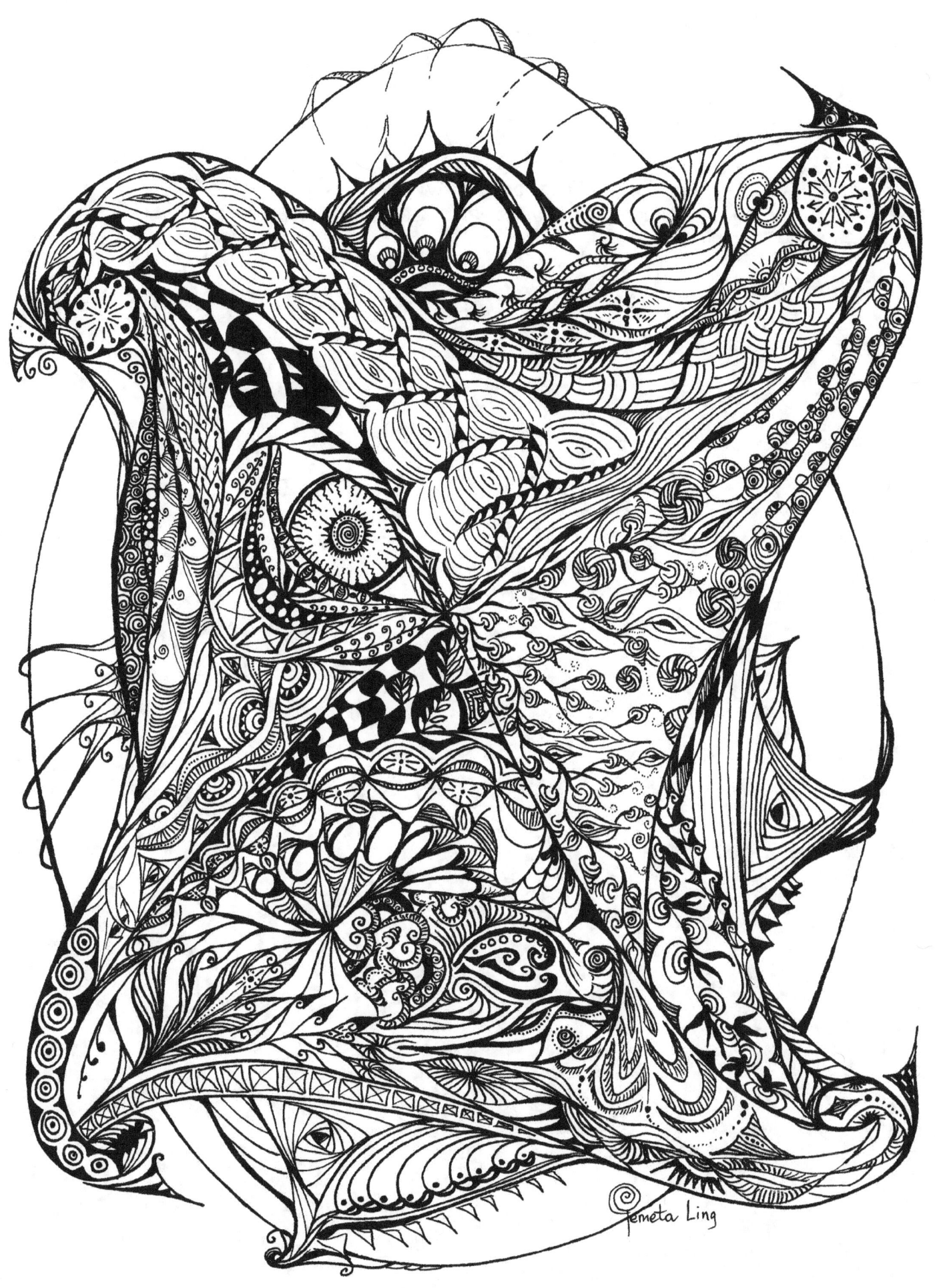

*Contributing Artist
Maria Wedel
Denmark*

Facebook : AMVWART
Facebook Group : ColorPagesOfAMVW/

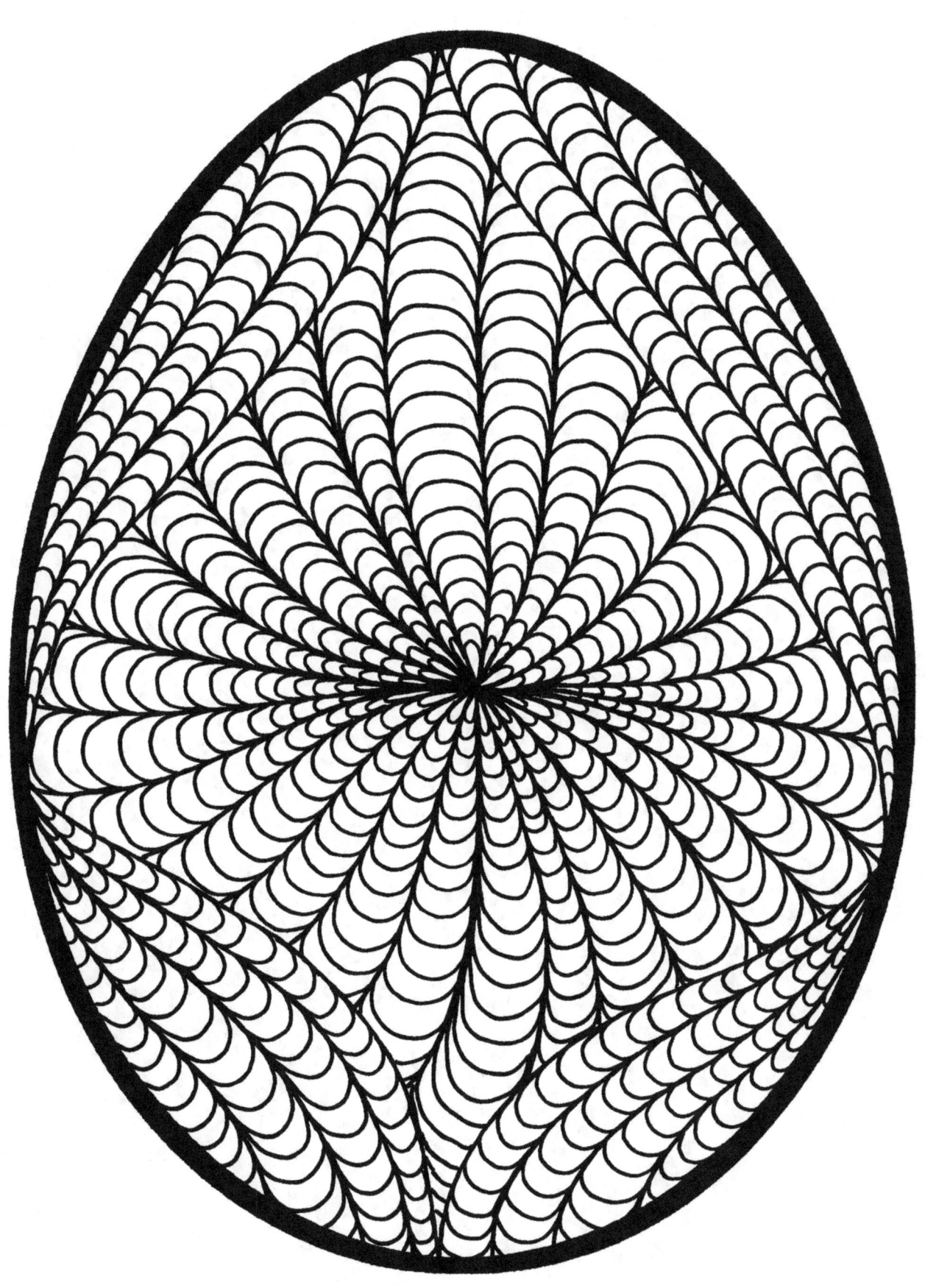

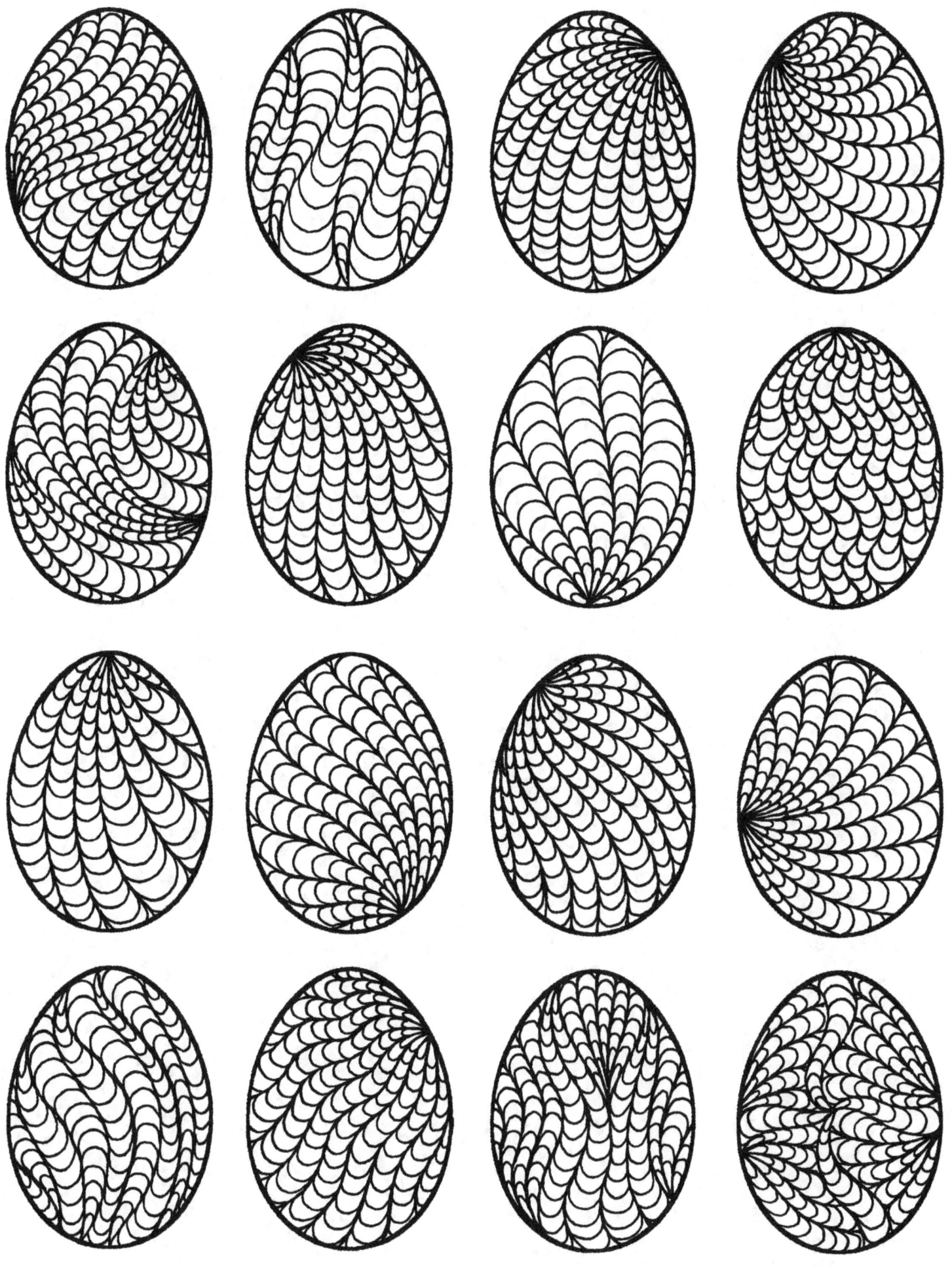

Drawn & colored

by

Les galaxies de 'Qi

Published by
"GDG"
Global Doodle Gems